I0449656

Thriving with ADHD:

30 Positive Parenting Techniques for Joyful Journeys

By
Erika Paz - MA, LPC, LCDC

About the Author

Erika commenced her professional journey in the realm of mental health in 2006, beginning in a crisis hotline call center. Since then, her career has blossomed through roles including case manager, social rehabilitation counselor, licensed substance abuse counselor, and psychotherapist licensed in Texas. Subsequently diagnosed with ADHD in 2005, she struggled with significant attention and focus issues during her pursuit of a master's degree.

Beyond her clinical roles, Erika is a seasoned psychotherapist, a devoted mother to a young son who shares her experience with ADHD, and she finds fulfillment in a harmonious family life alongside her husband.

In her therapeutic practice, Erika judiciously employs humor as a tool, drawing upon her own resilience in confronting personal challenges. She frequently invokes a poignant Freudian insight: "Words have a magical power." Firmly rooted in the principles of self-awareness, self-help, and self-discipline, she passionately advocates for their transformative potential.

This book is dedicated to empowering parents by imparting tools and strategies to foster the thriving of youth and teens with ADHD. Erika invites readers on a journey imbued with optimism, harnessing both her professional expertise and personal insights to navigate the landscape of ADHD with joy and resilience.

Disclosure

The names of individuals and identifying details used in this book have been changed to protect the confidentiality and privacy of the clients whose histories and experiences are presented. Any resemblance to actual persons, living or dead, is purely coincidental.

We have taken great care to ensure that the stories shared in this book do not reveal the identities of the individuals involved. The purpose of changing names and certain identifying characteristics is solely to safeguard the anonymity of our clients and to uphold the principles of confidentiality and ethical practice in our field.

Thank you for your understanding and respect for the privacy of those whose stories are shared within these pages.

Contents

Introduction

Welcome to a journey that's both heartwarming and challenging—a trek that we'll take together to unlock the potential in every child with ADHD. This book is for the compassionate, proactive learners among us who are striving to make a difference. You might be feeling overwhelmed by the constant influx of advice from well-meaning friends, the myriad online resources, and conflicting expert opinions. Maybe you're concerned about the idea of medication and how it fits into your child's life. You're not alone, and that's exactly why this book is here— to provide clear, actionable strategies to help your child flourish.

In a world buzzing with information, it's easy to get lost. We often find ourselves swimming in a sea of dos and don'ts, trying to figure out the best route forward. Here, we break it down for you. Our goal is simple: to give you practical tools that fit seamlessly into your day-to-day routine. We'll discuss effective discipline methods, how to build strong relationships, and the importance of creating structure and routines. The aim is to turn challenges into opportunities for growth—not just for your child, but for the entire family.

Think of this book as a roadmap. Each chapter is designed to guide you through a different yet crucial aspect of raising a child with ADHD. From understanding what ADHD really is, to learning positive parenting principles, to building solid relationships, and much more. We'll blend humor, real-life narratives, and instructional advice to keep things engaging and relatable.

Why humor, you ask? Because sometimes laughter really is the best medicine. Parenting, in any form, is stressful. Add ADHD to the mix, and it can sometimes feel like you're balancing on a tightrope. Humor helps us lighten up, laugh at ourselves, and take the edge off. While the journey you're on is serious and filled with emotional ups and downs, finding moments of levity can make it a lot more bearable.

While this book is filled with practical advice, it's not about following a rigid "one-size-fits-all" plan. Every child is unique, and what works for one might not work for another. That's why flexibility is key. Take what resonates with you, adapt it to fit your needs, and don't be afraid to experiment. The ultimate goal is to empower you with the knowledge and tools to help your child succeed.

Let's face it: there's no magic pill or quick fix. But there is hope. And the more you understand ADHD, the better equipped you'll be to help your child navigate their unique challenges and strengths. Whether you're a parent, a caregiver, or a teacher, the information in these pages is designed to support you in making practical, lasting changes.

As we delve into strategies for building strong relationships, you'll learn how to foster effective communication, emotional connections, and trust and respect. Effective discipline strategies covered later will help you implement positive reinforcement, understand natural consequences, and establish healthy boundaries. This book will also cover how to support your child academically, enhance their social skills, boost their self- esteem, and manage their emotions.

Medication is often a topic filled with questions and concerns. We provide a balanced view, exploring various options, their pros and cons, and how to work effectively with healthcare providers. Physical activity and its many benefits will be covered in-depth, giving you ideas for fun, engaging ways to integrate movement into your child's life.

Family dynamics play a crucial role in the life of a child with ADHD. We'll guide you through choosing a therapist and effective family therapy techniques. By sharing inspirational success stories from real families, we hope to offer not just guidance but also a sense of community and shared experience.

Life with a child who has ADHD can be demanding, but it is also incredibly rewarding. It's about finding that balance, embracing the rollercoaster of emotions, and celebrating every small victory. Through all these pages, remember that you're doing amazing work. Your love, patience, and commitment make a world of difference. So, take a deep breath, and let's embark on this journey together.

Are you ready to transform challenges into opportunities and learn how to help your child shine? Let's get started.

Chapter 1:
Understanding ADHD

ADHD is like that eccentric artist friend everyone's got—full of quirks and unpredictability, yet profoundly unique. This chapter unravels the complexities of ADHD, and trust me, it's a bit like peeling an onion— layer by layer, tear by tear. We'll start by digging into what ADHD actually is, cutting through the jungle of myths that make it seem like a modern-day boogeyman. We'll get into the nitty-gritty of how the ADHD brain operates, and spoiler alert, it's way more interesting than a standard brain. As we explore these topics, remember that understanding ADHD is the first step to providing effective support and solutions. This journey might make you chuckle, scratch your head, or even sigh in relief, but it'll always keep you intrigued.

What is ADHD?

ADHD, which stands for Attention Deficit Hyperactivity Disorder, is a neurodevelopmental condition that affects both children and adults. It's characterized by patterns of inattention, hyperactivity, and impulsivity that interfere with functioning or development. You might notice children with ADHD having trouble paying attention, frequently daydreaming, or being unable to sit still. Adults, on the other hand, might struggle with managing time, staying organized, or maintaining focus.

This condition isn't a one-size-fits-all scenario. People with ADHD present a variety of symptoms, and they can be classified into three types: inattentive type, hyperactive-impulsive type, and combined type. The inattentive type displays symptoms like an inability to pay close attention to details or frequently losing things necessary for tasks. The hyperactive- impulsive type might show excessive fidgeting, talking incessantly, or impatience. The combined type, which is the most common, includes symptoms from both categories.

Despite common misconceptions, ADHD is not a result of bad parenting or a lack of discipline. Instead, it's rooted in the brain's structure and chemistry. Researchers have found differences in brain regions that are involved in attention and executive function among those with ADHD. Neurotransmitters such as dopamine play a crucial role, which is why some medications for ADHD target these chemicals to alleviate symptoms.

Early diagnosis and treatment are essential. According to the Centers for Disease Control and Prevention (CDC), about 6.1 million children in the United States have been diagnosed with ADHD at some point. However, it's not only a childhood disorder; many adults continue to experience symptoms. For adults, untreated ADHD can lead to difficulties in personal relationships, employment, and mental health.

It's important to recognize that ADHD exists on a spectrum. Some individuals may have mild symptoms that are just a bit of an inconvenience, while others might face severe challenges that significantly impact their everyday life. Understanding where someone falls on this spectrum can help in tailoring support and interventions to their specific needs.

Parents often grapple with a whirlwind of emotions upon learning their child has ADHD. Fear, confusion, and sometimes relief at having an explanation for their child's behaviors are common reactions. Coping with the diagnosis involves educating oneself, seeking support, and understanding that while ADHD poses unique challenges, it also comes with its own set of strengths and talents. Many individuals with

ADHD are creative, energetic, and capable of hyper-focus on topics they are passionate about.

But why does ADHD occur? The exact cause isn't fully understood, but it's believed to be a combination of genetic, environmental, and neurological factors. Family studies have shown that ADHD can run in families, indicating a genetic component. Environmental factors, such as exposure to lead or maternal substance use during pregnancy, might also play a role, though these are less established.

Understanding ADHD also entails debunking some myths. One common misconception is that ADHD is overdiagnosed, especially in boys who are simply "being boys." In reality, girls often go undiagnosed because their symptoms might be less disruptive or manifest differently, such as through inattentiveness without hyperactivity. Additionally, ADHD isn't something that children can simply outgrow. While some may experience a reduction in symptoms as they age, many continue to face challenges into adulthood.

The landscape of ADHD management has evolved. Treatment approaches can be multifaceted, including behavioral therapies, medication, lifestyle changes, and educational support. Each child's or adult's treatment plan should be individualized, considering their unique profile and needs.

Behavioral therapy is often recommended as a first line of treatment, especially for young children. It involves training for parents to manage children's behaviors through positive reinforcement and structured routines. Cognitive-behavioral therapy (CBT) can also be beneficial for older children and adults by helping them develop coping strategies and change patterns of thinking.

Medication can be a controversial topic, but it's often an effective tool for managing ADHD symptoms. Stimulant medications, like methylphenidate and amphetamines, are the most commonly prescribed and have a significant body of research supporting their efficacy. Non-stimulant medications are also available for those who may not respond well to stimulants or have contraindications.

Engaging in lifestyle changes, such as incorporating physical activity and establishing consistent routines, can further support individuals with ADHD. Regular exercise has been shown to improve attention and reduce hyperactivity and impulsivity. Creating structured routines helps manage time and stay organized, which are common challenges for people with ADHD.

Educational support is crucial. Children with ADHD might benefit from individualized education plans (IEPs) or 504 plans, which provide accommodations to help them succeed in school. These might include extended time on tests, preferential seating, or breaks during long tasks.

In conclusion, ADHD is a complex condition that requires a comprehensive understanding and a supportive approach. By recognizing the symptoms, causes, and treatment options, parents, educators, and healthcare providers can work together to help individuals with ADHD thrive. Remember, having ADHD doesn't diminish one's potential; it's about harnessing strengths and addressing challenges with compassion and knowledge.

Common Myths and Misconceptions

When it comes to understanding ADHD, myths and misconceptions can muddy the waters, causing confusion, misjudgment, and even stigma. One prevalent misconception is that ADHD isn't a real disorder. Some folks believe it's an excuse for bad behavior, when in reality, ADHD is a well- documented neurodevelopmental disorder. Scientific research has shown that it involves differences in brain structure and function. The sunshine and rainbows version of ADHD might suggest that kids just need to "try harder" or that they're simply "lazy", but this couldn't be farther from the truth.

Another stubborn myth is the idea that ADHD only affects children. Yes, ADHD is often first diagnosed in childhood, but it's a lifelong condition. Many adults live with the challenges of ADHD, sometimes without even knowing it. The symptoms might evolve over time, but they don't vanish when someone hits adulthood. So, if Aunt Susan thinks you should've "outgrown" it by now, she's just confusing age with cure.

Then there's the misconception that ADHD is just about hyperactivity. While it's true that hyperactivity is one of the hallmark symptoms, not everyone with ADHD bounces off the walls. There are actually three types of ADHD: predominantly inattentive, predominantly hyperactive- impulsive, and combined type. Someone with inattentive type might be dreamy, easily distracted, or forgetful, without the hyperactive behavior. This variation often leads to underdiagnosis, particularly in girls, who are more likely to exhibit inattentive symptoms.

A surprising misconception is that ADHD is the result of bad parenting. Mothers and fathers are frequently blamed for their child's ADHD behaviors, leading to a lot of unfounded guilt and stress. The reality is that ADHD is a complex interaction of genetics, environment, and neurological factors. No amount of perfect parenting can change the underlying brain structures associated with ADHD!

Medication myths are also rampant. Some believe that ADHD drugs like Ritalin or Adderall will turn their children into "zombies." While it's true that finding the right medication and dosage can take time, when properly managed, medication can dramatically improve quality of life for individuals with ADHD. They're not meant to dull personalities but to help manage symptoms. Parents often worry about dependency, but with conscientious medical supervision, the benefits often outweigh the risks.

Let's not forget the myth that people with ADHD can't focus on anything. It's more accurate to say they struggle with regulating attention. This means they might hyperfocus on things that interest them, sometimes to the exclusion of everything else. Picture a child who can't tear themselves away from building an elaborate LEGO city but can't focus on their math homework. This doesn't mean they're incapable of concentration; it just plays out unpredictably.

There's also the misconception that only boys have ADHD. Boys are more frequently diagnosed, but girls have ADHD too. Their symptoms often manifest differently, like being quietly inattentive instead of overtly hyperactive. This difference has led to many girls being misdiagnosed or overlooked entirely, perpetuating the myth that ADHD is a "boy's disorder."

Schools often contribute to misconceptions as well. Some educators might mistake ADHD symptoms for mere behavioral issues, labeling kids as troublemakers. They may not understand the cognitive challenges these children face and thus misinterpret their actions. Effective communication and collaboration with educators can help correct these misconceptions and provide a more supportive educational environment.

Another outdated belief is that ADHD is a reflection of intelligence. Some people assume that a child with ADHD can't be smart or successful. In fact, ADHD affects people of all intelligence levels. Many individuals with ADHD are highly creative and intelligent, often thinking outside the box in ways others might not. The challenge lies in helping them harness their unique strengths.

Some people think that diet alone can cure ADHD. While a healthy diet can play a role in managing symptoms and overall well-being, it's not a standalone cure. Supplements, special diets, and avoiding certain foods might help to an extent, but they aren't a substitute for a comprehensive treatment plan, which could include therapy, behavioral strategies, and potentially medication.

Lastly, the myth that ADHD is overdiagnosed looms large. Critics argue that too many kids are being labeled with ADHD when they're just being kids. This perspective overlooks the rigorous diagnostic criteria and the thorough evaluations by trained professionals. Misdiagnosis and overdiagnosis can happen, but it doesn't negate the real and significant struggles faced by those genuinely dealing with ADHD.

In busting these myths, we hope to clear the fog that often surrounds ADHD. Recognizing these misconceptions is a step towards better understanding and more effective support for children dealing with ADHD. Dispelling these myths can foster a more compassionate, informed, and proactive community, ready to support and uplift those facing the unique challenges of ADHD.

The ADHD Brain

Understanding ADHD starts with understanding the brain. The brain of someone with ADHD works differently from those without this condition —it's not a matter of broken circuits, but rather a case of varied wiring. This unique wiring affects attention, impulse control, and executive functioning, creating both challenges and unexpected strengths. What's fascinating is how these brain differences carve out the vivid landscapes of everyday life, making each experience distinct for those with ADHD.

In many ways, the ADHD brain is like an orchestra without a conductor. Imagine the horns blaring, the strings plucking at will, and the percussion striking discordant beats. Each section of the brain plays a crucial role, but without a unifying force to bring harmony, the result can be overwhelming. This metaphor helps illustrate how ADHD impacts processes like task management, emotional regulation, and focus. The prefrontal cortex—the area responsible for these executive functions— often operates differently in those with ADHD.

One key area affected by ADHD is the neurotransmitter system, which includes chemicals like dopamine and norepinephrine. These chemicals play a significant role in transmitting messages between neurons, influencing motivation, pleasure, attention, and focus. In the ADHD brain, dopamine levels can be lower, making it challenging to maintain focus and complete tasks. It's like trying to tune into a radio station with signals constantly fluctuating—achievable but sometimes frustratingly elusive.

Genetics also play a crucial role in shaping the ADHD brain. Studies suggest that ADHD can run in families and is often inherited from parents. However, it's not just nature at play; nurture and environmental factors also contribute to how ADHD manifests. Understanding these influences can help in developing more personalized and effective strategies for managing ADHD symptoms.

Interestingly, the ADHD brain is often capable of "hyperfocus" on tasks or activities that are particularly engaging. This characteristic challenges the misconception that ADHD means a lack of focus overall. Rather, it's a matter of irregular focus—extreme concentration on certain tasks and difficulty maintaining attention on others. This duality can be both an asset and a challenge, depending on the situation.

Another aspect to consider is how the ADHD brain handles time management, often perceiving time differently. This can lead to difficulties with planning, forecasting, and meeting deadlines. It's similar to viewing the world through a distorted lens, where some moments feel elongated while others whiz by in a blink. Recognizing this time perception issue opens the door to developing specific strategies that help align the ADHD brain with everyday demands.

The brain's reward system is also significantly impacted by ADHD. Conventional rewards or motivations may not always work as intended. This is why strategies that might work for neurotypical brains—such as setting long-term goals or even simple sticker charts—often fall flat. Immediate, concrete rewards tend to be far more effective, aligning better with the ADHD brain's craving for instant gratification.

Emotionally, the ADHD brain can be a rollercoaster. Shifting moods, intense emotional responses, and a propensity for impulsive actions are common. Emotional regulation often requires extra effort and understanding. It's important to remember that these intense emotions are not a failing but a crucial component of the ADHD landscape. Strategies that incorporate mindfulness and coping techniques can be instrumental in navigating these emotional challenges.

Furthermore, sensory processing in the ADHD brain can differ. Some may be hypersensitive to environmental stimuli like bright lights or loud noises, while others may seek out sensory experiences, craving tactile or auditory input. This sensory variability requires tailor-made approaches for each individual, emphasizing the importance of personalized environments and routines.

Working memory, or the brain's ability to hold and manipulate information over short periods, is another area where ADHD makes its mark. Imagine trying to juggle while riding a unicycle—tasks that require holding multiple pieces of information can become overwhelmingly complex. For parents and caregivers, understanding this limitation is pivotal in crafting techniques that break down tasks into more manageable steps.

On the brighter side, the ADHD brain is often brimming with creativity and innovative thinking. This unique cognitive wiring allows for "out-of- the-box" perspectives, making individuals with ADHD excellent problem solvers and imaginative creators. When harnessed correctly, these creative abilities can lead to extraordinary achievements and breakthroughs.

Another strength lies in resilience. Many individuals with ADHD develop a robust sense of perseverance and determination precisely because they've had to navigate a world that often doesn't understand them. This resilience, when matched with the right support systems, can become one of their greatest assets.

Finally, understanding the ADHD brain provides key insights into the importance of connection and support. Relationships built on empathy, respect, and patience can make a significant difference. They serve as a buffer, allowing those with ADHD to thrive despite their challenges. Real progress and transformation become possible when caregivers, educators, and peers unite in understanding and supporting the unique ADHD brain.

While this chapter offers a glimpse into the intricacies of the ADHD brain, subsequent chapters will delve into how to leverage this understanding into actionable strategies for daily life. From effective discipline techniques to fostering positive relationships and creating supportive routines, the upcoming sections promise to equip you with tools to help children with ADHD succeed. By embracing the distinctive wiring of the ADHD brain, we can unlock a world of potential and possibilities.

Chapter 2:
Positive Parenting Principles

In the whirlwind of raising children with ADHD, it's easy to get caught up in the challenges and forget the incredible power of positivity. Positive parenting isn't just a feel-good concept; it's a transformative approach grounded in both science and practice. From reframing how we look at behaviors to setting the right expectations, applying these principles can create a nurturing and structured environment where your child can thrive.

So, what does positive parenting look like in action? First off, it's about speaking the language of encouragement. Instead of focusing on what your child is doing wrong, emphasize the things they're doing right. If they managed to sit through a homework session without fidgeting too much, that's a victory worth celebrating! It's these small acknowledgments that build confidence and show your child that they're more than their ADHD diagnosis.

The foundation of positive parenting involves setting realistic expectations. This can be particularly tricky because every child with ADHD is different. What's easy for one child might be nearly impossible for another. For instance, while one child might readily complete a math worksheet, another might struggle to sit still long enough to get through one problem. Tailoring your expectations to fit your child's unique capabilities can reduce frustration for both of you.

The Power of Positivity

Positive reinforcement goes a long way. It doesn't just mean giving a reward every time your child does something right but creating an environment where positive behaviors are naturally encouraged and nurtured. Think about it in terms of a garden. You wouldn't yell at flowers to make them grow; instead, you provide water, sunlight, and nutrients.

Similarly, offering praise, rewards, and even just your attention can make positive behaviors bloom.

Using positive language is also key. Instead of saying, "Stop running around in the house," try "Let's walk in the house, please." It might seem like a minor shift, but it makes a big difference. You're telling your child what you want them to do instead of just what you don't want.

Setting Realistic Expectations

Setting realistic expectations involves understanding your child's strengths and weaknesses. Start by observing your child closely. Do they have trouble focusing on tasks, but excel when activities are hands-on? Are mornings particularly tough for them? Use these observations to set goals that are achievable. For example, if mornings are hard, don't expect your child to whip through their morning routine without a hitch. Break down tasks and offer plenty of encouragement along the way.

Incorporate structured choices to empower your child. For instance, if getting dressed is a daily battle, allow them to choose between two outfits. This small decision can make them feel more in control and reduce resistance.

It's also helpful to communicate expectations clearly and consistently. Create visual schedules and use simple, direct language to explain tasks. Consistency is reassuring for children with ADHD; they thrive when they know what to expect.

Fostering a Growth Mindset

A growth mindset, popularized by psychologist Carol Dweck, emphasizes the belief that abilities and intelligence can be developed through dedication and hard work. This concept is incredibly powerful for children with ADHD, who often face more criticism and setbacks than their peers.

Encourage your child to see challenges as opportunities to grow rather than insurmountable obstacles. When they struggle with a task, praise their effort, not just the outcome. This teaches them that persistence pays off. Statements like "You worked so hard on that puzzle! I'm proud of you for not giving up" build resilience and a love for learning.

Reframe failures as learning experiences. If a particular strategy for tackling homework doesn't work, discuss other approaches together. This shift from a fixed mindset ("I can't do this") to a growth mindset ("I can't do this yet") can transform how your child perceives their abilities.

Building Emotional Intelligence

Often, the emotional aspect is overlooked, but emotional intelligence is crucial. Teaching your child to recognize and express their feelings can be a game-changer. Start with basic emotions like happiness, sadness, and anger, and gradually introduce more complex feelings like frustration and excitement.

Use everyday moments as teaching opportunities. If your child is upset because they struggled with a task, acknowledge their feelings. "I can see you're frustrated. Do you want to talk about it?" This validates their emotions and opens the door to problem-solving together.

Model emotional regulation by staying calm during conflicts. Your behavior provides a template for how to handle strong emotions. If you do lose your cool, it's also an opportunity to show how to make amends. Apologize and explain how you plan to manage your feelings better next time.

Implementing positive parenting principles in a household with an ADHD child takes time, patience, and a lot of trial and error. But the rewards—a more harmonious family life, a confident and resilient child—are well worth the effort. By keeping positivity, realistic expectations, and a growth mindset at the forefront, you're not just managing ADHD; you're fostering an environment where your child can flourish.

The Power of Positivity

Too often, the challenges of parenting a child with ADHD can overshadow the many positives each day brings. However, in the realm of positive parenting principles, the power of positivity cannot be overstated. Children with ADHD often face a world that's quick to criticize and slow to praise. They're bombarded with instructions on what not to do, rather than being encouraged for the things they get right. As a parent, integrating positivity into your daily interactions can make a substantial difference in your child's life.

Positivity begins with your mindset. If you constantly focus on the negatives and mishaps, you're more likely to feel stressed and overwhelmed—and so will your child. On the flip side, if you adopt a positive outlook, you'll notice improvements in your emotional well- being and, consequently, your parenting effectiveness. It's about seeing the glass half full, celebrating small victories, and understanding that progress might come in increments. Your attitude toward challenges will influence your child more than you might realize.

Start by ensuring that praise is specific and meaningful. General comments like "good job" are nice, but they don't tell your child what they did right. Instead, try something more specific, such as, "I noticed how you focused on your homework today, that was impressive!" This type of praise helps your child understand their achievements and encourages repetition of positive behaviors. It's also more likely to boost their self- esteem, leading to a domino effect of confidence and further positive actions.

Another key aspect of positivity is maintaining a positive tone of voice, even during corrections. This doesn't mean you should never address misbehavior, but how you address it matters. Focus on what you want to see rather than what you're displeased with. For instance, instead of saying, "Stop running around the house," you could say, "Let's walk safely inside and save the running for outside." It seems cliche and repetitive, however; this subtle shift in language can make a world of difference to a child with ADHD, who might already feel constantly reprimanded.

Creating a positive home environment also involves showcasing positive behavior yourself. Children are keen observers and often mimic what they see. Demonstrate self-compassion when you make mistakes, highlighting the importance of learning from errors rather than feeling defeated by them. When you handle stress calmly and use positive self-talk, you provide a blueprint for your child to follow in their own challenging moments.

It's crucial to create opportunities for success. Sometimes, children with ADHD might struggle in traditional settings and face frequent setbacks. To counterbalance this, find activities where they can excel and shine. Whether it's a sport they're good at, a hobby they're passionate about, or creative pursuits like drawing or music, offering these outlets can build their confidence and give them something to look forward to.

Family activities that emphasize fun and positivity also contribute significantly. Regularly scheduled family nights, whether it's for board games, movie marathons, or outdoor adventures, can foster a sense of belonging and security. These moments not only act as stress relievers but also fortify the bonds you share as a family. Laughing together, celebrating together, and simply enjoying each other's company is an antidote to the everyday stresses that life brings.

Moreover, teaching children to reframe their own thoughts can be incredibly powerful. If your child says, "I'm bad at math," guide them to instead say, "I'm still learning math, and I'm getting better every day." This shift encourages a growth mindset, promoting resilience and perseverance. It's not about pretending challenges don't exist, but rather about recognizing that effort and a positive outlook are critical components of overcoming those challenges.

As much as we'd like to protect our children from adversity, it's inevitable. What you can do, however, is help them develop a toolkit for dealing with these adversities constructively. Encourage them to view setbacks as temporary and solvable, fostering a spirit of optimism and can-do attitude. This mindset will not only help them in childhood but will serve them well throughout their lives.

Incorporating the power of positivity also means celebrating strengths. Every child has unique talents and abilities, and those with ADHD are no different. Celebrate these strengths and make a big deal out of their achievements. This might mean keeping a chart of accomplishments on the refrigerator or verbally acknowledging their hard work at dinner. These positive reinforcements can build a sense of pride and motivation.

Finally, don't forget to take care of yourself. Parenting can be exhausting, and it's easy to let your own well-being slide. A positive mindset is easier to maintain when you're well-rested, eating healthily, and taking time for activities you enjoy. When you take care of yourself, you're better equipped to care for your child. Your positivity can then become a beacon that guides your child through their own challenges.

The power of positivity lies in its ripple effect. By embedding positive parenting principles into your daily routine, you're not only fostering a supportive and encouraging environment for your child but also equipping them with invaluable life skills. Positivity paves the way for resilience, confidence, and an overall sense of well-being that can transcend the challenges of ADHD and help your child thrive now and in the future.

Setting Realistic Expectations

As we dive into the world of positive parenting principles, it's essential to ground ourselves in the concept of setting realistic expectations. It's easy to get swept away by optimism, especially when we're fueled by a desire to do our best for our children. But remember, positive parenting isn't about expecting perfection; it's about appreciating progress and striving for consistent, meaningful improvements.

First and foremost, let's talk about the importance of setting achievable goals. We're all guilty of imagining our kids transforming overnight into model children, but reality often paints a different picture. If your child struggles with ADHD, the journey is even more complex. It's unfair to expect instant results when there's so much to navigate, from understanding their unique brain functions to implementing effective strategies. Instead, focus on small, incremental changes that build up over time. Celebrate those baby steps, because they lead to significant strides in the long run.

This brings us to the big picture: why set realistic expectations in the first place? Unrealistic expectations can lead to frustration, disappointment, and even resentment—for both you and your child. When we expect too much too soon, we set ourselves up for a cycle of guilt and blame. By contrast, realistic expectations foster patience and resilience, creating a more nurturing environment for our kids to grow and thrive. It's not just about reducing stress for the parents; it also helps children build confidence when they meet attainable goals.

Let's get a bit nerdy for a moment and talk brain science. Children with ADHD often have neurobiological differences that make certain tasks more challenging. For instance, impulse control, attention span, and emotional regulation can be areas where they struggle. Expecting a child with ADHD to suddenly sit still for long periods or exhibit perfect behavior at a family gathering is not just unrealistic; it's setting them up for failure. Instead, acknowledge these challenges and adjust your expectations accordingly. You'll find that a little empathy goes a long way.

Now, it's time to get tactical. How do you actually set these realistic expectations? One effective approach is the SMART goal framework. SMART stands for Specific, Measurable, Achievable, Relevant, and Time- bound. By setting goals that fit these criteria, you can ensure they are within reach and can be tracked effectively. For example, instead of saying, "I want my child to do better in school," consider a SMART goal like, "I want my child to complete their homework for 30 minutes every school night for a month." This way, both you and your child have a clear, manageable objective to work toward.

Another technique involves breaking down larger tasks into smaller, more manageable chunks. This can particularly help children with ADHD who might feel overwhelmed by big projects or changes. For instance, instead of expecting your child to clean their entire room, start with specific areas like the desk or bed. Gradually, you'll see progress without the drama that often accompanies larger tasks.

While we're on the topic of expectations, don't forget about the importance of flexibility. Life is unpredictable, and strict adherence to a plan can sometimes do more harm than good. Be prepared to adapt your expectations as situations evolve. If your child has an off day or if external circumstances change, it's okay to adjust your goals. Flexibility doesn't mean lowering your standards; it means being realistic about what's achievable under varying conditions.

We also need to consider the role of communication in setting these expectations. Have conversations with your child about what you both hope to achieve. This aligns your efforts and ensures that your child understands what is expected of them. Encouraging their input can also lead to more buy-in, making it more likely that they'll put effort into meeting these goals. Moreover, involving them in the process teaches them valuable skills in self-assessment and goal-setting.

Setting realistic expectations isn't just about academics or chores; it's equally crucial in social and emotional realms. Social interactions can be particularly challenging for children with ADHD. They might struggle with reading social cues or controlling their impulses during play. Expecting flawless social behavior isn't fair. Instead, work on specific skills like taking turns or using polite language incrementally. Each small improvement is a step in the right direction.

Remember, setting realistic expectations also means being kind to yourself. Parenting is hard work, and it's even more demanding when you're managing ADHD symptoms. It's okay to feel frustrated or overwhelmed—what matters is how you handle those emotions. Cut yourself some slack and recognize that you're doing your best. When you set realistic expectations for yourself, you'll find it easier to stay patient and positive with your child.

Finally, let's talk about what happens when expectations aren't met. It's natural to feel disheartened, but consider each setback as a learning opportunity rather than a failure. Analyze what went wrong and adjust your approach. Was the goal too ambitious? Did external factors interfere? Share these reflections with your child, framing them as part of the ongoing journey rather than the end of the road.

In essence, the art of setting realistic expectations is about balancing optimism with pragmatism. It's about understanding and accepting where your child is while keeping an eye on where you want them to be. By setting achievable goals, being flexible, and maintaining open communication, you'll create a supportive environment where your child can grow and flourish. And in the grand scheme of things, isn't that the ultimate goal?

Fostering a Growth Mindset

In the grand scheme of positive parenting principles, fostering a growth mindset in children with ADHD is paramount. It's about nurturing the belief that abilities and intelligence can be developed through dedication, hard work, and learning from mistakes. Now, let's dive deep into practical ways to foster this mindset in your children.

First off, it's essential to understand that setbacks and challenges are an inevitable part of life, more so for children with ADHD. Instead of shielding them from difficulties, encourage them to view these obstacles as opportunities to grow. When a child struggles with a homework assignment, for instance, shift the focus from simply getting the correct answer to valuing the process of learning. Praise the effort, perseverance, and strategies they employ rather than just the outcome.

This approach not only helps in diminishing the fear of failure but also instills resilience. Encourage them by recounting your own experiences with challenges and failures. Discussing how you overcame obstacles and what you learned along the way can provide them with a powerful, relatable perspective.

Language plays a critical role here. Replace phrases like "You're so smart" with "You worked really hard on this". The latter underscores effort as the pathway to achievement. When your child sees their hard work paying off, they start associating effort with success.

Another key aspect is setting realistic, yet challenging goals. This could be academically, socially, or in any area where your child faces difficulties. Work with them to set short-term and long-term goals. Celebrate small milestones along the way, reinforcing that progress is a series of small steps forward, often accompanied by occasional steps back.

It's also important to create a learning-rich environment. Provide them with a variety of resources like books, puzzles, and games that challenge their cognitive and emotional skills. Make learning a fun and integral part of their daily life, rather than a chore or obligation. Positivity towards learning in the environment at home can significantly influence their attitude towards growth and improvement.

Modeling a growth mindset yourself is powerful. Children are keen observers and often mirror the attitudes and behaviors of their parents. Show them how you tackle your learning experiences and setbacks. Verbalize your thought process in front of them. For instance, if you're trying to solve a problem at work, explain how you're approaching it, the strategies you're considering, and how you're learning from any mistakes made along the way.

Failure is often seen as a negative experience, but in the context of a growth mindset, it becomes a learning opportunity. Make it clear that failures are not to be feared but to be expected and learned from. Share stories of famous personalities who faced multiple failures before achieving success. This can inspire them to persist despite immediate setbacks.

Incorporate a daily reflection time where both you and your child discuss the day's challenges and what was learned from them. This practice not only reinforces the idea that learning is ongoing but also strengthens your relationship and opens lines of communication.

Furthermore, encourage curiosity and questions. Children with ADHD might have varied interests and asking questions propels them to think critically and explore deeper. Support their inquisitive nature by answering their questions to the best of your ability and exploring unknowns together. This fosters a love for learning and builds an inquisitive mindset.

When it comes to skills, teach them that mastering new skills takes time and practice. Whether it's learning to play a musical instrument, mastering a new sport, or improving their reading skills, emphasize that growth occurs gradually, through persistent effort and practice. Highlighting stories of incremental progress can serve as powerful motivators.

Consider collaborating with educators and specialists who understand the nuances of ADHD. They can offer additional strategies that align with what you're fostering at home. Consistency between home and school can be incredibly beneficial. Most importantly, reassure them constantly that they are valued and loved, regardless of their struggles or setbacks.

The role of peer influence shouldn't be underestimated either. Encouraging your child to engage with peers who also value growth and learning can provide them with additional models and reinforcements of a growth mindset. Arrange playdates or group activities where they can observe and practice persistence, effort, and learning from mistakes in a social context.

It's vital to recognize and address the emotional aspects involved. Children with ADHD may experience heightened sensitivity to failure and criticism. Be gentle and patient if they show signs of frustration or defeat. Acknowledge their feelings and provide comfort and reassurance, reiterating the importance of effort and learning over immediate success.

Introducing mindfulness practices can be beneficial as well. Techniques such as deep breathing, meditation, or journaling can help them manage stress and stay focused on their growth journey. Mindfulness helps in fostering a calm and composed mindset, allowing them to tackle challenges more effectively.

In conclusion, fostering a growth mindset in children with ADHD is an enriching process that involves consistent effort, encouragement, and collaboration. It's about instilling values of perseverance, resilience, and lifelong learning. As parents, your role is to guide, support, and inspire. Remember, it's about progress, not perfection. Every small step forward is a victory worth celebrating.

Chapter 3:
Building Strong Relationships

Building strong relationships is the cornerstone of helping children with ADHD flourish. It might seem daunting at first – how do you connect deeply with your child amid the daily chaos and distractions? But, it's both possible and essential. It starts with understanding the foundation of effective communication and emotional connection.

It's essential to talk with your child, not at them. Effective communication involves not just speaking but also listening – really listening. That means putting down your phone, making eye contact, and showing genuine interest in what your child has to say. Ask open-ended questions to get them to open up, instead of just yes or no answers. For example, "What was the best part of your day?" can lead to a more meaningful conversation than "Did you have a good day?"

Communication is more than just words; it includes tone, body language, and timing. If your child is upset, it might not be the best time to have a serious discussion. Instead, wait until they've calmed down and are more receptive. Remember, the goal is to connect, not to correct.

Emotional connection goes hand-in-hand with communication. Your child needs to feel understood and valued. This emotional bond is nurtured through empathy. Try to see the world through their eyes, understand their struggles, and celebrate their successes, no matter how small they may seem.

Validation is key. When your child shares their feelings or frustrations, acknowledge them. Say things like, "I can see why that would be upsetting," or "It sounds like you had a tough time with that." These simple affirmations can make a big difference in how understood they feel.

Trust and respect are pillars of any strong relationship, and it's no different with your child. To build trust, be consistent in your actions and words. Follow through on promises and be reliable. If you say you'll do something, make sure you do it. Consistency helps your child feel safe and secure, knowing they can depend on you.

Respecting your child means valuing their opinions and feelings, even if you don't always agree. Give them choices and opportunities to make decisions, fostering a sense of autonomy and self-worth. For instance, let them choose between two options for dinner or decide on a weekend activity. Involving them in decision-making shows that their preferences matter.

In addition to respecting their choices, acknowledge their individuality. Each child is unique and has their own strengths and challenges. By focusing on their strengths and helping them navigate their challenges, you can build a stronger, more supportive relationship.

Another practical approach is to spend quality time together. This doesn't mean just being physically present but engaging in activities that both of you enjoy. Whether it's playing a game, cooking together, or simply going for a walk, these moments create lasting bonds and memories.

Lastly, don't forget to take care of yourself. Parenting, especially when dealing with ADHD, can be exhausting. Make sure you have your support system – friends, family, or support groups – to lean on. Taking care of your mental and emotional health enables you to be the best parent you can be, nurturing a loving and robust relationship with your child.

So, foster open communication, build emotional connections, establish trust and respect, and cherish the quality time you spend together. These efforts may seem small but are monumental in shaping a supportive and loving environment where your child can thrive.

Effective Communication

Communicating effectively is a cornerstone of building strong relationships, especially when it comes to children with ADHD. It involves more than just exchanging words; it's about connecting in ways that foster understanding, trust, and cooperation. Effective communication can transform your interactions, making everyday conversations more meaningful and reducing misunderstandings.

Imagine this: you're trying to get your child to complete their homework, but every time you bring it up, it turns into a battle. Instead of making demands or raising your voice, try using a calm and positive tone. Begin by acknowledging their feelings. You might say, "I know homework isn't the most fun thing to do, but let's see if we can get through it together." This approach not only shows empathy but also sets a collaborative tone right from the start.

One effective strategy is to use clear and concise language. Children with ADHD often struggle with instructions that are too lengthy or complex. Break down tasks into smaller, manageable steps. For instance, instead of saying, "Clean your room," say, "Please put your toys in the bin first." This way, the child knows exactly what is expected of them without feeling overwhelmed.

Active listening is another crucial component of effective communication. It involves truly hearing what the other person is saying without interrupting or planning your response while they're speaking. Show that you are engaged by maintaining eye contact, nodding, and providing verbal feedback like, "I see," or "That makes sense." When your child feels heard, they're more likely to open up and share their thoughts and feelings.

Effective communication is also about timing. Choose moments when both you and your child are relatively calm and focused. Trying to have a meaningful conversation when they're upset or distracted is unlikely to yield positive results. It's okay to say, "I can see you're upset right   now. Let's talk about this after dinner," giving them time to cool down and approach the conversation with a clearer mind.

Humor can be a powerful tool in communication as well. Sharing a laugh can break the tension and make challenging topics more approachable. If your child is struggling with a particular task, a little joke or a funny anecdote can lighten the mood and make them more receptive to your guidance.

Non-verbal communication plays a significant role too. Your body language, facial expressions, and tone of voice can convey messages just as strongly as your words. A gentle touch on the shoulder or a warm smile can reassure your child that you are on their side.

Think about creating a special signal or code word to use when emotions run high. This can be a non-intrusive way for your child to express that they need a moment to regroup. For example, if they say "Time-out", it could mean they need a few minutes of silence to collect their thoughts. This empowers them to communicate their needs without escalating the situation.

Empathy is fundamental in effective communication. Try to see the world from your child's perspective. Understanding that their experiences and challenges are different from yours helps you communicate in a more supportive and constructive manner. Simple phrases like, "I can see this is really tough for you," can validate their feelings and show that you truly car e.

Conflict resolution is an area where effective communication shines. When disagreements arise, focus on the issue at hand rather than resorting to blame or criticism. Use "I" statements to express your feelings without making the other person defensive. For example, say, "I feel frustrated when the toys are left out because I trip over them," rather than, "You never clean up your toys."

Consistency is key. If you establish certain communication protocols, stick to them. Whether it's weekly family meetings, daily check-ins, or specific times for discussing important matters, maintaining regularity helps set expectations and builds a routine that children with ADHD often find comforting.

Remember, effective communication is a two-way street. Encourage your child to express themselves and take their opinions seriously. Ask open- ended questions like, "What did you enjoy about your day?" or "How can I help you with that problem?" These types of questions invite more than a yes or no answer and encourage deeper conversations.

Ultimately, the goal of effective communication is to build a stronger, more trusting relationship with your child. It's about creating an environment where they feel safe, understood, and valued. Through clear instructions, active listening, empathy, and humor, you can navigate the complexities of ADHD and create a positive and supportive dynamic in your household.

Communication isn't just about solving problems; it's also about celebrating successes. Make sure to regularly acknowledge and praise your child's efforts and achievements. Positive reinforcement can go a long way in motivating them and reinforcing good behaviors. A simple "Great job on finishing your homework!" can have a significant impact.

With patience and practice, effective communication becomes second nature. It helps diffuse conflicts, builds emotional connections, and fosters mutual respect. By incorporating these strategies into your daily routine, you'll not only improve your interactions with your child but also set the foundation for a lifelong, loving relationship.

The Importance of Emotional Connection

In the whirlwind of daily life, especially when navigating the complexities of ADHD, it's easy to overlook the fundamental need for emotional connection. But connecting on this deeper level is not just nice to have— it's essential. For children with ADHD, feeling understood, valued, and loved lays the groundwork for everything else. Emotional connections act like the glue that binds relationships, ensures effective communication, and fosters mutual respect. When children feel emotionally connected, they're more likely to respond to guidance, engage positively in activities, and even manage their ADHD symptoms better.

Let's consider a typical scenario. Imagine coming home from a long day at work to find your child restless and unfocused. It's tempting to jump straight into discipline mode—directing tasks, issuing commands, and generally trying to restore order. But what if you paused for a moment and connected emotionally? Instead of saying, "Why haven't you done your homework?" you might say, "Hey, it looks like today was a tough day. What's going on?" This simple shift acknowledges the child's feelings and opens up space for a meaningful conversation.

Emotional connections thrive on empathy and understanding. Try to see the world from your child's perspective. For example, a child with ADHD may struggle with tasks that others find easy, leading to feelings of frustration and inadequacy. By recognizing and validating these emotions, you create an environment where your child feels safe to express themselves. A statement like "I see you're really frustrated with this math problem. How about we tackle it together?" can go a long way in building trust.

Kids with ADHD often experience emotional highs and lows more intensely than their peers. This heightened emotional sensitivity means they are more affected by the dynamics within their relationships. When they feel emotionally connected to their caregivers, it provides a buffer against the challenges they face daily. So, if a child knows they can count on you for emotional support, they're more likely to handle difficult situations with greater resilience.

Effective emotional connection isn't one-size-fits-all. Children have unique ways of feeling loved and secure. Some may need physical affection, like hugs or a reassuring pat on the back. Others might respond better to verbal affirmations or quality time spent together. Figuring out your child's "love language" can be a game-changer. It makes your efforts to connect more impactful and tailored to their specific needs.

Building an emotional connection requires consistency. Sporadic attempts to engage emotionally might not yield long-term benefits. Children need to know that their emotional safety is a priority at all times, not just when things are going smoothly. Commit to frequent check-ins, even if it's just a few minutes of genuine, focused attention each day. These small moments accumulate and create a reservoir of emotional trust.

Another powerful tool for creating emotional bonds is storytelling. Sharing personal stories—be it about your own day or memories from your childhood—provides a context for your child to understand and relate to you. It's a two-way street. Encourage your child to share their experiences as well. Storytelling can make abstract concepts more relatable and provide a platform for discussing emotions and challenges in a non-threatening way.

Listening actively is crucial. It's easy to fall into the trap of 'hearing' without truly 'listening'. Active listening involves more than just nodding along; it requires you to engage, reflect, and respond appropriately. Use phrases like "What I hear you saying is..." or "It sounds like you're feeling..." to show that you're genuinely in tune with your child's thoughts and feelings. This not only validates their experience but also encourages an open and ongoing dialogue.

While building emotional connections is vital, it's equally important to manage your own emotional health. Parenting a child with ADHD can be demanding, and emotional burnout is a real risk. It's okay to seek support —whether from friends, family, or professional counselors. When you are emotionally balanced, you're in a better position to offer your child the stability they need.

Laughter and fun are also integral to emotional connection. Shared activities that bring joy can strengthen the bond between you and your child. Whether it's playing a game, going for a hike, or even baking cookies together, these experiences create positive memories and reinforce the idea that your relationship is not solely about rules and responsibilities.

Sometimes, the road to an emotional connection can be rocky. Misunderstandings and conflicts are inevitable, but they can also be opportunities for growth. How you handle these moments can teach your child valuable lessons about problem-solving and emotional regulation. Approach conflicts with a mindset focused on resolution rather than blame. Phrases like "Let's figure this out together" or "What can we do differently next time?" foster a collaborative atmosphere.

Physical presence matters too. Being there, especially during times of distress, underlines your commitment to the relationship. Even if you can't offer a solution immediately, your mere presence can be incredibly comforting. Sit with your child, hold their hand, or simply be there in silence. These actions speak volumes about your unwavering support and love.

It's essential to celebrate the small victories. Acknowledge not just the big milestones, but also the minor achievements and efforts your child makes. These moments of recognition can significantly boost your child's self- esteem and reinforce their emotional connection to you. Statements like "I'm proud of how hard you worked on that project" or "I appreciate your effort in managing your emotions today" can be incredibly validating.

In a world that often feels chaotic and unpredictable, emotional connection offers a haven of stability. It's the bedrock upon which you can build effective communication, trust, and ultimately a strong, supportive relationship. For children with ADHD, knowing they have a parent or caregiver who understands and cares deeply about their emotional well- being can make all the difference.

So, the next time you find yourself caught up in the hustle and bustle, remember that the most impactful thing you can do is to pause and connect emotionally. It might just be the anchor both you and your child need to navigate the waters of ADHD together.

By making emotional connections a priority, you're not only addressing the immediate challenges but also laying the foundation for a lifelong relationship based on love, trust, and mutual respect. And that, more than any strategy or technique, is what will help your child thrive.

Trust and Respect

Building a strong relationship grounded in trust and respect with a child who has ADHD isn't just beneficial; it's paramount. Yet, many parents find themselves at a loss on how to nurture these critical elements. Sure, you can set boundaries and enforce rules, but the core foundation of any relationship, especially one involving a child with

ADHD, lies in trust and respect. This section will delve into why these two pillars are essential and provide practical strategies to help you cultivate them.

First and foremost, trust is a two-way street. Many parents expect their children to trust them implicitly, but forget that earning a child's trust is equally important. Trust provides a sense of safety and stability that children with ADHD often crave amidst the chaos. To build trust, consistency is key. When you say you're going to do something, follow through. If you promise to take your child to the park after school, don't back out unless it's absolutely unavoidable. And if you must cancel, explain why openly and honestly. The transparency helps build trust as your child sees you're reliable and sincere.

Respecting your child's individuality is another foundational aspect. ADHD often brings unique challenges, but it also brings unique strengths. Celebrate these strengths and respect their individuality. For instance, your child might struggle with sitting still but excel in creative projects or hands-on activities. Recognize and respect these unique traits. Avoid comparing them to others, especially to siblings or peers who don't share their struggles. Such comparisons can erode self-esteem and create a sense of inadequacy.

Now, emotional validation plays a significant role in fostering respect. Kids with ADHD often feel misunderstood or judged. Listen actively when they express themselves. Maintain eye contact, nod, and use verbal cues to show you're engaged. When they share their feelings, acknowledge them. Phrases like "I understand why that made you upset," or "That must have been frustrating," go a long way in making your child feel heard and respected. Always aim to validate their emotions, even if their behavior needs addressing. This distinction helps them understand that while certain actions may not be acceptable, their feelings are always valid.

Mutual respect also entails setting realistic expectations and boundaries. Respect your child's developmental stage and tailor your expectations accordingly. It's essential to understand that children with ADHD may not meet conventional milestones at the same pace as their peers. That doesn't mean they won't achieve them; it just means they might take a different path to get there. By setting achievable goals and providing the support they need, you show respect for their unique journey, helping reinforce their confidence and trust in you.

Another key approach to building trust and respect is through effective communication. Avoid using negative language or punitive measures to get your point across. Instead, frame your requests and directives in a positive, instructional manner. For instance, instead of saying "Don't yell," try "Please use a quieter voice." This not only makes the instruction clear but also respects their capacity for understanding and improvement. On the flip side, always be open to their perspectives as well. Ask for their thoughts and feelings on family rules or routines. While you remain the authority, showing that their input matters fosters a more respectful relationship.

Consistency in discipline is another cornerstone of fostering trust and respect. While this might seem challenging, especially with the unpredictability that often accompanies ADHD, it's non-negotiable. Create a set of clear, consistent rules and enforce them fairly. When rules are broken, apply predetermined consequences without anger or frustration. Your child needs to understand that rules exist for their well-being and that breaking them leads to predictable outcomes. Equally, praise and reward good behavior consistently. This balance reinforces the idea that you're fair and trustworthy.

Respect also involves understanding and accommodating sensory needs. Children with ADHD often have heightened sensory sensitivities. They might be overstimulated by loud noises, bright lights, or certain textures. Creating a sensory-friendly environment at home, such as a quiet space where they can retreat, shows empathy and respect for their needs. It's also useful to work with educators to ensure they receive similar accommodations in school.

Lastly, respect involves modeling the behavior you want to see. Children learn about respect not just from directives but from observing how you interact with others. Show kindness, patience, and respect in your interactions with family members, friends, and even strangers. Use polite language, show appreciation, and practice active listening. When your child sees these behaviors consistently, they're more likely to emulate them.

Building trust and respect with a child who has ADHD might require extra effort, but the rewards are well worth it. A relationship based on these principles will not only help your child thrive but also strengthen the entire family dynamic. Consistency, empathy, effective communication, emotional validation, and mutual respect are the key ingredients. Implementing these strategies can turn the everyday challenges associated with ADHD into opportunities for growth and connection.

Just remember, building trust and respect doesn't happen overnight. It's an ongoing process that requires patience, understanding, and a willingness to adapt. Your efforts in cultivating these values will pay off, creating a supportive environment where your child feels secure, valued, and respected. This foundation will not only help them succeed academically and socially but will also set the stage for a lifetime of strong, healthy relationships.

Chapter 4:
Creating Structure and Routine

In the whirlwind of parenting a child with ADHD, creating structure and routine can feel like trying to tame a tornado. Yet, it's one of the most impactful strategies that you can implement to help your child succeed. Think of routine as the strong framework that provides stability and predictability in your home. It acts as an anchor, helping your child feel more secure in the midst of internal chaos.

First things first, let's talk about consistency. When you create a consistent environment, you're giving your child a sense of reliability. Knowing what to expect helps reduce anxiety and buildup confidence. Yes, it's easier said than done. Life happens, and no one is perfect, but aiming for consistency as much as possible can be a game-changer.

Start by developing daily schedules. These schedules should be detailed yet flexible enough to accommodate the unpredictable nature of life. Define timeframes for waking up, meals, school, homework, play, and bedtime. You don't need to be a drill sergeant, but try to stick to these times as closely as possible. Visual aids like charts or checklists can make schedules more engaging for your child. Use colorful markers, stickers, or drawings to make it interactive and fun.

Another essential aspect is creating transition techniques. Transitions are typically tough for kids with ADHD. Moving from one activity to another can be jarring and lead to meltdowns. Easing these transitions can involve using countdowns, timers, or simple verbal cues. For instance, giving a ten-minute, five-minute, then one-minute warning before changing activities helps prepare your child mentally. Using tools like visual timers or even a smartphone alarm with a fun sound can make transitions smoother.

Consistency isn't just about time; it's also about context. Try to maintain a consistent environment in your home. This means having designated areas for specific activities. Establish a quiet, distraction-free zone for homework and a different space for playtime. Creating these boundaries helps your child associate specific areas with particular tasks, making it easier for them to transition from one activity to another.

Routines don't have to be stiff. Build flexibility into your structure by allowing for breaks. Breaks are particularly important for kids with ADHD to prevent burnout and manage restlessness. These "brain breaks" should be short but frequent and filled with a fun, engaging activity. A quick dance session, a stroll outside, or a few minutes of doodling can do wonders.

Sometimes, routines can become monotonous for your child, which can lead to resistance. Keep them involved in creating the schedule. When they have a hand in planning their day, they are more likely to stick to it. Ask for their input on what activities they'd like to include, or let them choose the order of some tasks. Giving them a sense of control can encourage participation and adherence.

Now, let's discuss communication. Clear communication plays a crucial role in implementing and maintaining routines. Use simple and concise language when explaining the schedule to your child. Over-complicating instructions can be overwhelming. Keep it straightforward: "First, we will finish homework, then we can play your favorite game."

Positive reinforcement should not be overlooked. Praise your child for sticking to the routine. Positive feedback can motivate them to continue following it. Rewards don't have to be extravagant. Sometimes, a simple "Great job!" or a high-five can make a big difference. Celebrate small victories and milestones to keep the momentum going.

Life is unpredictable, and sometimes routines will be disrupted. That's okay. The key is to get back on track as soon as possible without guilt or frustration. Life is filled with teachable moments, and showing resilience in adapting to changes can be a valuable lesson for your child.

Lastly, don't forget self-care. Managing a household with a child with ADHD can be demanding, and you need to be at your best to provide the support they need. Make sure to carve out time for yourself, even if it's just a few moments of quiet in the morning or a walk in the evening.

Creating structure and routine isn't about eliminating spontaneity. It's about finding a balance that works best for your family. By providing stability through a well-thought-out routine, you can help your child navigate their world with greater confidence and less stress.

The Role of Consistency

Consistency is, without a doubt, the cornerstone of creating effective structure and routine, especially for children with ADHD. Imagine trying to assemble a puzzle with ever-changing pieces; that's what life can feel like for a child with ADHD. Consistent routines and expectations act like the fixed edges of a puzzle—they provide a reliable frame that helps everything else fall into place.

When kids know what to expect, they're less likely to feel anxious and more likely to succeed. Consistency helps manage the symptoms of ADHD by providing clear boundaries and expectations. If they know bedtime is always at 8 PM, there's less negotiating, less stalling, and ultimately, less stress for everyone involved. It's not about being rigid; it's about being reliably predictable.

Think of consistency like a guiding star. It doesn't move, it doesn't waver, and it provides a steady point of reference in an otherwise chaotic sky. For children with ADHD, whose internal worlds can be in constant flux, external consistency can offer a much-needed sense of stability. It builds a foundation upon which they can construct their daily lives, ensuring they have a safe space to return to when things become overwhelming.

For example, establishing a morning routine can work wonders. If every day starts with waking up at the same time, followed by brushing teeth, getting dressed, and eating breakfast, it sets a positive tone for the day. Even something as simple as laying out clothes the night before can save precious minutes in the morning and reduce the chances of a meltdown.

The same principle applies to school work. A consistent homework schedule can make a world of difference. Designate a specific time and place for homework each day. This doesn't just help the child to focus; it also signals that schoolwork is a priority and part of their daily responsibilities.

Consistency isn't just for the kids—parents, this one's for you, too. When you're consistent in your parenting, it builds trust. If you say, "No TV until homework is done," and stick to it, your children learn that your word means something. This leads to a trusting relationship where the kids feel secure knowing the rules won't change arbitrarily. It also helps in reinforcing good behavior patterns when kids know exactly what's expected of them.

But let's be real—life happens. There will inevitably be days where routines go out the window, and that's okay. The goal isn't perfection but predictable reliability. Maybe you're traveling, or the family has a special event. The key during these times is to maintain as much of the routine as possible. Bring familiar items, stick to meal and sleep schedules as closely as you can, and try to prepare your child for any changes ahead of time.

Consistency also means co-parents should be on the same page. One parent can't be the strict one while the other is lenient; this creates confusion and inconsistency. Communication between co-parents is crucial. Discuss routines, rules, and expectations, and make a unified plan. This way, children know they can't play one parent against the other for their benefit.

A good strategy is creating visual cues and charts. Visual schedules are amazing tools because they provide a tangible reference for what's expected. These can be simple charts showing morning and evening routines, or more elaborate calendars that lay out the week's activities. The visual element helps children understand and remember these routines, and checking off tasks can be immensely satisfying for them.

While we talk about consistency, it's also important to understand that it doesn't mean we shouldn't be flexible. Children with ADHD are not robots, and life is unpredictable. There will be times when bending the rules a little is the best course of action for everyone's sanity. The key is to understand when flexibility is okay and when it disrupts the structure too much.

Consistency in discipline is equally important, but that's a topic we'll dive deeper into later. For now, understand that fair and predictable consequences teach children accountability. If the consequence for not doing homework is losing some screen time, that needs to be the case every time. Random or disproportionate consequences only add to the confusion.

You can also make consistency fun and engaging. Incorporate rewards and positive reinforcement to maintain enthusiasm around routines. For instance, using a reward system like star charts for completing daily tasks can encourage kids to stick to their routines. Make a big deal out of small accomplishments—it goes a long way.

Social stories can be another useful tool. These short stories illustrate and reinforce expected behaviors and routines in a way that's relatable to children. They can be tailored to specific situations, like a trip to the dentist or the first day at a new school, helping to prepare your child for what's coming next.

Consistency is like planting a seed. With time, care, and a predictable watering schedule, it grows into a strong, reliable tree. Parents often marvel at the progress their children make when consistent routines are well established. They're not just surviving—they're thriving. And that's the ultimate goal, isn't it? To help our children not just cope with their ADHD but to actually flourish in spite of it.

In conclusion, the role of consistency cannot be overstated when creating structure and routine for children with ADHD. It's the bedrock that supports all other strategies and interventions. It makes expectations clear, reduces anxiety, builds trust, and ultimately, helps children succeed. While it's challenging to maintain in our ever-changing world, a consistent approach pays dividends in the long run, creating a nurturing environment where children with ADHD can truly thrive.

Developing Daily Schedules

Creating a structured daily schedule can feel like a Herculean task when you're juggling the demands of a household, work, and a child with ADHD. But here's the not-so-secret secret: it doesn't have to be perfect. It just has to work. And believe me, even a flexible, lightly enforced routine can work wonders for kids with ADHD.

Let's start with mornings. We all know mornings can be chaotic. From lost shoes to forgotten homework, that short span before the day really kicks off can make or break everything. A simple morning routine could mean the difference between everyone begrudging out the door and starting the day with a small victory. So, kick it off with time blocks. Say, 15 minutes for getting dressed, 10 minutes for breakfast, 5 minutes for brushing teeth, and so on. It sounds rigid, but the actual times aren't as important as the consistency of the activities.

Setting up visual or auditory cues can be a game-changer. Imagine alarms on your child's watch or smartphone that gently nudge them to move to the next task. Even a colorful chart on the fridge with stickers for completed activities can do wonders for motivation. Kids with ADHD often struggle with internalizing time, so external cues become incredibly helpful.

Mid-morning routines will vary greatly depending on whether your child is at school or at home. Either way, ensure some room for physical activity. Five minutes of jumping jacks, a brisk walk, or even a quick dance session can help reset their focus and burn off excess energy.

Next up, let's tackle after-school routines. Homework time needs to be predictable. Choose a consistent time and a designated, distraction-free space. Before diving into the books, it's wise to have a brief decompression period. This could be a snack, a chat about their day, or even some quiet time. The goal here is to transition smoothly.

Post-homework, incorporate downtime that allows for free play, or other enjoyable activities they choose. This period of the day should be somewhat unstructured to give them a sense of autonomy. Unlike other times of the day where structure is key, a little flexibility here can keep them engaged and interested.

Dinner time is another cornerstone. Making dinner a family affair can bring consistency and connection. Encourage kids to help set the table or even do some simple cooking tasks. This can help them feel involved and important, plus it teaches responsibility. Just like mornings, having clear expectations can prevent this vital time from slipping into chaos. And try to end dinner with a ritual, maybe it's sharing "highs and lows" of the day, or five minutes of family reading time.

Let's move on to evening routines. Start wrapping up the day with calm activities. High-energy events close to bedtime can wreak havoc on sleep schedules. Reading, puzzles, or simple crafts work well. Keep bedtime consistent, not just in the hour but also in the rituals that lead up to it. A warm bath, followed by reading a book, then bed. Rinse and repeat.

Before saying goodnight, it's worthwhile to peek into their room together to ensure a clean and clutter-free space. Less visual clutter means a less distracted mind and hopefully, a better night's sleep. Creating a serene atmosphere can dramatically improve the quality of their sleep, which affects the next day's routine.

You might be wondering, what about weekends? Ah, weekends. The double-edged sword of freedom and chaos. Keeping some structure even on the weekends provides a sense of stability. Yes, allow for later wake-up times, but don't abandon all routine. Plan family activities or outings, and keep mealtimes relatively steady. Even on more relaxed days, the rhyme of routine offers a comforting predictability.

It's crucial to involve your child in the planning process. When they have a say, they're much more likely to engage willingly. Sit down together and discuss what needs to be done and when. Offer them choices within the structure. For example, "Would you like to do your homework right after school or after a 30-minute break?" Giving them some control helps in fostering a sense of responsibility and independence.

One trick that seasoned parents swear by is "brain breaks." Short, frequent breaks can be pivotal in maintaining focus throughout the day. It's not rocket science; even a simple break can make all the difference. Whether it's stretching, a quick snack, or a few moments of deep breathing, these breaks act as little reset buttons to reboot attention and energy levels.

And here's something to remember: routines are living documents. They aren't carved in stone and need to adapt as your child grows and their needs change. Be ready to tweak them occasionally based on what's working and what's not. Flexibility, within the confines of structure, is your best friend here.

Account for downtime within their schedule for creative activities, hobbies, and relaxation. Let's not forget that children, just like adults, need time to unwind. Slotting in activities that they love and look forward to acts as a fantastic motivator and makes the tricky parts of the day more manageable.

Positive reinforcement is another key component. Celebrate when the schedule is followed well. This doesn't mean you need a grand parade; simple acknowledgments like "Great job sticking to your morning routine today!" go a long way. Rewards systems—like earning tokens for a bigger weekend treat or extra screen time—can also be effective, but keep them balanced to avoid over-reliance.

Working closely with educators can bring uniformity between home and school routines. Sharing your child's home routine with their teachers and understanding the school's schedule helps in creating a seamless flow for your child. Consistent routines across environments make it easier for them to adapt and thrive.

It's also wise to prepare for disruptions. Life happens—sickness, family emergencies, events. Preparing your child in advance about deviations from the usual schedule can help ease transitions. For instance, "Tomorrow, we'll be skipping the afternoon homework time because of auntie's birthday party." It's about setting the expectation so they aren't blindsided by changes.

Lastly, always keep communication open. Check-in daily, or even multiple times a day, to gauge how they're feeling about their schedule. Encourage them to voice any difficulties they're facing and work on solutions together. Active dialogues help cultivate a sense of partnership and trust, making them more likely to embrace and follow the routines you establish.

Each child is unique, so be patient and observe what works best for your family. Developing daily schedules is not just about filling in blocks of time, but about creating a rhythm that resonates with your child's pace and needs. Take it one step at a time, and remember, perfection is not the goal —progress is.

Transition Techniques

Establishing structure and routine is critical for children with ADHD, but transitions between activities can be particularly challenging. These moments of change can feel abrupt, causing anxiety and behavior disruptions. Fortunately, with a few strategic techniques, you can smooth these transitions and make the day flow more calmly.

One effective approach is using visual and auditory cues to signal an upcoming transition. For example, set a timer for five minutes before the change. The consistent sound of the timer becomes a predictable signal that it's time to switch tasks. You might also use visual schedules with pictures or icons to represent different activities. This way, children can see what's coming next, reducing anxiety about the unknown.

Verbal warnings are another powerful tool. Give a gentle reminder five minutes before an activity ends, followed by a two-minute warning. This helps set expectations and allows children to mentally prepare for the change. Make your warnings simple and clear, such as, "In five minutes, we will start cleaning up to get ready for dinner."

Implementing a consistent routine around transitions can help. For instance, if your child struggles switching from playtime to homework, create a routine that includes a calming activity between the two, such as five minutes of deep breathing or a quick snack. This acts as a buffer and makes the transition less jarring.

Offering choices also empowers children and can make transitions smoother. Instead of saying, "It's time to stop playing with Legos," you might say, "Do you want to put away your Legos now, or in five minutes?" Giving children a sense of control over their choices can reduce resistance and enhance cooperation.

Another tactic is to use countdowns. For some children, visual timers like hourglasses or digital countdown clocks can be very effective. Watching the time tick down to a transition can provide a concrete understanding of passing time. This visual prompt reinforces the predictability of the schedule.

One often overlooked but crucial factor is the emotional state of the child during transitions. Recognize and validate their feelings. If they're particularly engaged in an activity, acknowledge it. "I see you're having a lot of fun building that tower. It can be hard to stop when you're having a good time." This acknowledgment can also make it easier for them to accept the transition.

Also, practice transitions during low-stress times. Rehearse and role-play different scenarios with your child. For example, simulate getting ready for school or an evening wind-down routine. This rehearsal can build familiarity and confidence, so actual transitions are less stressful.

Incorporating movement can help ease transitions, too. Engaging in a physical activity, even just for a minute or two, can help children release pent-up energy. You might incorporate a fun, brief exercise like jumping jacks or a quick dance party before transitioning to a more sedentary activity.

Maintaining clear, calm, and consistent communication is vital. Rather than rushing or yelling, use a reassuring tone of voice. Consistent language and calm demeanor can make transitions feel safe and less overwhelming.

Consider the environment as well. The physical space can significantly influence how transitions are perceived and managed. Create clear zones for different activities, like a designated homework area that's separate from play areas. This spatial distinction helps children mentally and physically prepare for the upcoming activity.

If a child has a particularly hard time with a specific transition, try to identify any underlying triggers. Is it a sensory issue? Are they hungry or tired? Addressing these basic needs can significantly improve how they handle transitions.

Incorporating predictable rituals around transitions can also be beneficial. A special song for clean-up time or a funny phrase every time you prepare for homework can make transitions more enjoyable and less monotonous.

Finally, it can be immensely helpful to involve the child in planning the routine. Allow them to have input on the schedule and discuss what types of transitions they find easiest or hardest. Engaging them in the process helps them feel more invested and can lead to better cooperation.

Remember, consistency is key. The more regularly you employ these techniques, the more they become second nature to your child. Over time, with patience and practice, transitions can become smoother and less stressful, freeing up more energy for both you and your child to enjoy the day.

Chapter 5:
Effective Discipline Strategies

When it comes to disciplining a child with ADHD, things can get tricky. The usual methods may not always apply, and constant trial and error can leave you feeling utterly exhausted. However, adopting effective discipline strategies tailored to the unique needs of your child not only brings harmony but also helps in nurturing their overall development.

First off, let's talk about positive reinforcement. It's one of the most effective strategies for managing the behavior of a child with ADHD. Rather than focusing on what they're doing wrong, highlight what they're doing right. Celebrate their small wins. Did they manage to put away their toys without being asked? Let them know you noticed. Did they finish their homework on time? Give them a high-five. Positive reinforcement builds their self-esteem and encourages them to repeat good behavior. Use a reward system, like stickers or extra playtime, to give them a tangible reason to keep up the good work.

On the flip side, we have natural consequences. No, this isn't about letting them run wild until they learn their lesson the hard way. It's about letting the consequences of their actions teach them. If they refuse to wear a coat on a cold day, they might feel chilly. Obviously, safety is paramount—so don't skip the coat if it's dangerously cold— but small inconveniences can be powerful teachers. Through natural consequences, children understand their actions on a deeper level.

It's important to set boundaries, and more importantly, to stick to them. Children with ADHD often struggle with impulsivity and lack of foresight, making clear boundaries a lifeline. Consistent rules provide them with a predictable framework within which they can operate safely. Be specific about what is acceptable and what isn't. Instead of saying "Be good," try "When we visit Grandma, I expect you to use your indoor voice and keep your hands to yourself." Once boundaries are set, be consistent in enforcing them. If bedtime is at 8:00 PM, it should always be at 8:00 PM—even on weekends.

Visual aids can work wonders. Use charts, checklists, or even colorful post-it notes. Visual cues provide constant reminders of what's expected. For example, a morning routine chart can help them remember to brush their teeth, get dressed, and pack their school bag without you having to remind them constantly. Some parents find using apps on tablets or smartphones useful for this, but good old pen and paper work just as well.

Communication is crucial. Make sure to praise their efforts and successes. Feedback should be immediate; waiting too long can dilute its impact. Use short, clear instructions and avoid long-winded explanations. "Clean your room" is better than "I need you to organize your toys, make your bed, and put your clothes in the hamper."

Another strategy is called "behavioral contracts." These are simple agreements between you and your child that outline the expected behavior and the associated rewards or consequences. Write it down and review it together. For instance, "If you do your homework for 30 minutes every day this week, you'll get to choose a movie to watch on Friday night." This method empowers them by giving them a sense of control over their actions and the outcomes.

Let's not overlook the importance of self-care for parents. Dealing with ADHD can be physically and emotionally draining. Make sure to carve out time for yourself. Whether it's a quick walk, a chat with a friend, or reading a book, self-care helps you recharge and approach discipline from a calm and composed state of mind.

Last but not least, keep humor in your toolkit. Laughter can defuse many a tantrum and lighten the mood, making discipline a less daunting task. Funny faces, silly voices—anything that gets a giggle and breaks the tension can be incredibly effective.

By using these discipline strategies, you pave the way for a more peaceful household, fostering an environment where your child feels understood, respected, and capable of meeting expectations. Although the journey might be bumpy, the rewards of seeing your child thrive make it 100% worth the effort.

Positive Reinforcement

Positive reinforcement is arguably one of the most effective discipline strategies, especially for children with ADHD. These kids often face a barrage of criticisms and corrections throughout their day, and it can be easy to focus on what they're doing wrong rather than what they're doing right. But here's the thing: children thrive on positive recognition. It boosts their self-esteem and encourages them to repeat the behaviors that get them that treasured pat on the back.

One of the primary benefits of positive reinforcement is that it helps create a more positive atmosphere overall. Instead of a constant cycle of reprimands and corrections, you build an environment where good behavior is noticed and celebrated. This shift doesn't just impact the child; it positively influences the whole family's dynamic. It's about creating a culture where positivity is the norm.

When using positive reinforcement, it's crucial to be specific about what behavior you're praising. Vague compliments like "Good job" are nice but not as effective as a specific comment like "I'm really proud of how you sat through your reading time today." Specificity helps kids understand exactly what they did right and encourages them to repeat that specific behavior.

It's important to remember that positive reinforcement isn't a one-size- fits-all strategy. Different children are motivated by different things. For some, verbal praise is enough; for others, tangible rewards like stickers or a small treat can be more motivating. The key is to understand what works best for your child and tailor your approach accordingly.

Now, before you start handing out rewards like candy, it's essential to strike a balance. The goal isn't to produce a generation of kids who expect rewards for every little thing they do. Think of positive reinforcement as a tool to highlight and encourage specific behaviors, especially those that might be challenging for a child with ADHD.

- **Verbal Praise:** As mentioned, verbal reinforcement can be very effective. Simple, yet heartfelt, affirmations can go a long way. Remember, it's the quality of praise that counts—not just its quantity.

- **Token Systems:** Create a system where children earn tokens or points for exhibiting desired behaviors. These tokens can be exchanged for rewards, like extra playtime or a small toy. The sense of accumulating something for a goal can be very motivating.

- **Charts and Stickers:** For younger children, sticker charts can be an engaging way to track their accomplishments. Every time they exhibit the desired behavior, they get a sticker. Watching the chart fill up can be a source of tremendous pride for them.

Positive reinforcement isn't limited to tangible rewards, either. Sometimes the most effective reinforcement is simply spending quality time with your child, giving them undivided attention as a reward. This forms a dual purpose: the child feels valued and the parent-child bond strengthens.

When implementing a positive reinforcement plan, consistency is key. Sporadic praise or rewards can lead to confusion and fail to establish a clear connection between the behavior and the outcome. It should be predictable enough that the child understands: when I do X, I will get Y.

Additionally, keep in mind that positive reinforcement can be a powerful tool outside of just "disciplinary" contexts. For instance, if a child is struggling academically, celebrating small achievements like completing homework on time can bolster their confidence and encourage them to keep at it.

While it's essential to focus on the positive, it's also crucial to be genuine. Children are remarkably adept at sensing insincerity. If you're showering praise just for the sake of it, without it being earned, it can lose its impact. Ensure that your praise is deserved and coming from a place of genuine appreciation for their efforts.

Also, don't be discouraged if the changes aren't immediate. Reinforcement takes time and persistence. You're not just working to change behaviors but also to rewrite the narrative your child holds about themselves. For children with ADHD, who often hear more about what they're doing wrong, this can be a game-changer.

The beauty of positive reinforcement lies in its adaptability. It's not restricted to parents and can be seamlessly integrated by teachers, caregivers, and even the kids themselves. Encourage them to notice and celebrate their own achievements. Self-praise can be a critical tool for building internal motivation and self-worth.

Finally, positive reinforcement helps in setting a hopeful tone for the future. When children with ADHD experience regular positive feedback, it helps them to internalize that they are capable and competent. This developing self-belief can lead to fewer behavioral issues as they feel increasingly secure and confident in their abilities and actions.

So, give it a try. Make positive reinforcement a staple in your disciplinary toolkit. It doesn't solve everything, but it can create an environment where positive behaviors are more likely to flourish. And let's face it, in the chaotic landscape of raising a child with ADHD, who couldn't use a bit more positivity?

Natural Consequences

When it comes to disciplining a child with ADHD, natural consequences can be an incredibly effective strategy. Many parenting books and experts will tell you that natural consequences help children learn about the real- world outcomes of their actions. While this general advice is well- intentioned, children with ADHD often need more guidance about these natural outcomes. Let's dive into the nuances to make this approach a bit more tailored to their unique needs.

Natural consequences are, in simplest terms, the outcomes that occur without parental intervention. If a child forgets their homework, the consequence is receiving a lower grade or having to face their teacher's disappointment. The child learns without you having to lay down arbitrary punishments. It's straightforward and makes sense. But, for kids with ADHD, the straight path isn't always the easiest or the most coherent one.

Why are natural consequences so effective? The direct relationship between action and result can be more impactful than any manufactured consequence. For example, leaving a bike out in the rain (and it subsequently rusting) teaches the importance of taking care of personal belongings far better than a lecture ever could. However, kids with ADHD might miss this cause-and-effect relationship unless we help them connect the dots.

Let's consider how we can scaffold these natural processes to make them digestible. Start with breaking down tasks and outcomes. If your child forgets their lunch, rather than swooping in to save the day, let them face the mild discomfort of being hungry for a few hours. But afterwards, discuss the experience with them: "How did you feel when you didn't have your lunch today?" Guiding them through this reflection helps in internalizing the lesson.

One key aspect of natural consequences is consistency. It's crucial to let the consequence flow naturally and not intervene too quickly. But also, consistency in follow-up discussions is essential. Providing a safe space to talk about what happened and how it made them feel is critical in helping them process the event. Using humor in these conversations can help ease the sting and foster a learning environment rather than one of mere punishment.

Sometimes, these natural consequences can seem harsh—especially when we love our kids and want to protect them from discomfort. But remember, the world itself won't always cushion their fall. By allowing our children to face the results of their actions in a controlled and loving environment, we're preparing them for real life. In the long run, they'll be better equipped to handle challenges independently.

It's essential to differentiate between natural consequences and punitive consequences. Natural consequences stem directly from the child's behavior, whereas punitive consequences are imposed by the parent. For parents of ADHD children, avoiding punitive measures and focusing on natural outcomes can prevent the power struggles ADHD kids often engage in. Remember, the goal is not to control but to teach.

Additionally, using natural consequences helps foster responsibility. For instance, if a child doesn't study for a test and performs poorly, the natural consequence is the bad grade, not a grounded weekend. We can encourage our children to see the link and understand that their efforts lead directly to their results. When these situations arise, sit down with them and discuss what strategies can be adopted next time to avoid a similar outcome. This promotes a growth mindset, encouraging improvement and learning from mistakes.

However, not all natural consequences are appropriate. Safety should always come first. If a natural consequence could potentially harm your child, it's vital to step in and prevent the situation. For example, if a child wants to touch a hot stove to see what happens, it's better to intervene and explain the severity of the consequence rather than letting them learn in a potentially harmful way.

When properly implemented, natural consequences can be a gentle yet powerful way to help children with ADHD understand the impact of their actions. They promote an invaluable sense of accountability without creating fear or resentment. Of course, natural consequences shouldn't exist in a vacuum. They should be part of a toolbox that includes other strategies like positive reinforcement and structured routines.

While it may be more challenging to use natural consequences with younger children or those with severe ADHD symptoms, it's entirely possible with patience and foresight. Start with small, manageable situations. Experiment with low-risk scenarios where the consequences are mild. As your child grows more accustomed to understanding these outcomes, gradually introduce more complex situations.

In family settings, consistency across all caregivers is crucial. Ensure that everyone, from parents to grandparents, understands the approach to natural consequences. Discuss and agree on scenarios where natural consequences will be allowed to play out. This unified front helps in reinforcing the learning process for the child.

Another aspect worth mentioning is the element of time. Children with ADHD often struggle with time management and future planning. They may not immediately connect a delayed consequence to their behavior. In such cases, it's helpful to provide immediate, verbal feedback linking the action to the consequence. This will help form a more concrete understanding and reinforce the learning process.

Take, for example, a child who consistently refuses to wear their coat in cold weather. A natural consequence would be feeling the discomfort of cold. The key here is to follow up—not just with "I told you so"—but with empathy. You might say, "It felt really cold outside without your coat, didn't it? Next time, how about we try to remember to wear it so you stay warm." This approach combines empathy, natural consequences, and guidance, making the learning process more comprehensive.

Using natural consequences isn't just an effective discipline strategy—it's a life skill. It teaches resilience, self-awareness, and emotional intelligence. When kids understand that they have control over their outcomes, they're more likely to take responsibility for their actions. This empowerment can be especially beneficial for children with ADHD, who often struggle with feelings of inadequacy or helplessness.

In summary, natural consequences work by allowing children to learn from the outcomes of their actions. For children with ADHD, this method is enhanced by supportive follow-up discussions, a consistent approach among caregivers, and attention to time management. The goal is to foster a sense of responsibility and resilience, paving the way for children to navigate the complexities of life with greater confidence and understanding.

Setting Boundaries

When it comes to raising children with ADHD, setting boundaries isn't just helpful—it's crucial. Boundaries offer a sense of security and clear expectations, which children with ADHD often need to thrive. Think of boundaries as the guardrails that keep a child on track, much like lane markers on a road. Sure, there might be some wobbling and touching the boundaries, but that's a part of learning and growing.

Let's get one thing straight: boundaries aren't about creating a rigid, military-like environment. Instead, they are about establishing a framework within which a child can navigate their world. Imagine trying to play a soccer game without any lines marking the field. It would be chaotic and confusing, right? The same principle applies here—boundaries help in avoiding confusion and chaos.

Boundaries provide consistency, which is often challenging but incredibly beneficial for children with ADHD. Knowing what's expected of them and having predictable consequences for actions can help these kids manage their environment more effectively. It creates a sense of reliability, where they understand that certain behaviors lead to certain results.

The first step in setting effective boundaries is to ensure they're clear and understandable. Vague rules are as good as no rules at all. For example, instead of saying, "Behave at the dinner table," specify what you mean: "Sit in your chair until dinner is over and speak in an inside voice." Kids with ADHD often need concrete guidelines rather than abstract concepts.

Another key factor is consistency. If a boundary is set, it needs to be enforced consistently. If inconsistency creeps in, it sends mixed signals. Think of it as reinforcing a muscle; the more you exercise it, the stronger it gets. Children will test boundaries—that's a given. It's how they learn the limits. By consistently upholding the boundaries, you offer a reliable framework for them to rely on.

Consequences play a pivotal role in the effectiveness of boundaries. It's essential to distinguish between punishment and natural consequences.
While punishment might deter unwanted behavior temporarily, natural consequences help children understand the real-world implications of their actions. For example, if they neglect their homework, the natural consequence might be a lower grade. This teaches responsibility and accountability far better than a time-out might.

However, the effectiveness of boundaries doesn't come just from the rules themselves but also from how they're communicated. Use positive language and frame boundaries in a way that feels supportive rather than restrictive. For instance, say, "Let's keep our toys in our room to keep the living room clean," instead of "Don't leave your toys here."

Empathy and understanding are crucial while setting boundaries. Kids with ADHD don't misbehave because they wish to; often, their actions stem from their impulsive nature. Addressing these issues with compassion rather than frustration can make a world of difference. Validate their feelings: "I see you're frustrated because you have to stay in your room to play. Let's talk about why this is important."

It's also important to involve your child in the boundary-setting process. When children are part of creating the rules, they're more likely to understand and respect them. Have a conversation about why certain boundaries are necessary and ask for their input. This not only makes them feel valued but also teaches negotiation and compromise—valuable life skills.

Reinforce the boundaries through repetition and reminders. Children with ADHD often need frequent reminders due to their distractibility. Visual aids can be especially helpful. Use charts, color codes, or even simple sticky notes to serve as continuous reminders of the rules and expectations.

Flexibility is another component not to be overlooked. While consistency is key, it's also crucial to be adaptable when needed. Life is unpredictable, and sometimes, strict adherence to a boundary might not be feasible. In such cases, explain why a rule is being bent momentarily and ensure it's understood as an exception, not a norm.

Let's talk about the role of positive reinforcement in setting boundaries. Positive reinforcement doesn't just emphasize what the child shouldn't do, but also what they're doing right. Rewarding positive behaviors can sometimes be more effective than punishing negative ones. This could be as simple as verbal praise, extra playtime, or a small reward tied to consistent good behavior.

The benefits of setting boundaries are substantial. Children with ADHD often struggle with executive functioning, which includes skills like memory, flexible thinking, and self-control. Clear boundaries aid in developing these skills over time, as they provide a practice ground for following guidelines and understanding consequences.

Boundaries also foster independence. In understanding what's acceptable and what isn't, children develop the ability to self-regulate, an invaluable skill as they grow older. This helps them make better decisions even when they aren't under direct supervision.

Another practical tip: monitor and adjust boundaries as needed. As your child grows, their needs and abilities will change. What was a necessary boundary at age five might not be as relevant at age ten. Regularly reassessing these boundaries ensures they remain effective and reasonable.

Lastly, remember that setting boundaries is not just limited to the child. Adults in the home should also model respecting boundaries themselves. Children often learn by imitation. When they see you respecting personal space, adhering to household rules, and valuing open communication, they're more likely to mirror these behaviors.

Building a consistent habit of setting and maintaining boundaries involves effort, patience, and a lot of love. It's a foundational element of effective discipline strategies, especially for children with ADHD. These guardrails you establish today will pave the way for a smoother, more predictable journey for both you and your child.

Chapter 6:
Supporting Academic Success

Sometimes, the classroom feels like a battleground for children with ADHD. With so many rules, schedules, and demands, it's easy for them to feel overwhelmed. But here's the good news: there are practical ways to support their academic success that don't require reinventing the wheel.

First things first, working with educators is crucial. Teachers can be your greatest allies if you approach the situation with collaboration in mind. Start by setting up a meeting with your child's teacher to discuss their specific needs. Be open about what works at home and be sure to ask for their observations in the classroom. It's not about pointing out flaws but about creating a unified support system. Teachers often have valuable insights and can offer helpful strategies, like seating arrangements that minimize distractions or recommending additional resources. The goal is to create a supportive, tailored academic environment.

Homework. Those seven letters can induce stress in any household, but it doesn't have to be a nightly struggle. Establish a consistent homework routine that includes breaks. Creating a quiet, distraction-free space can also do wonders. Get creative! Use timers to break tasks into manageable chunks, and don't shy away from using rewards for completion. Sometimes, a five-minute game or a sticker chart is all it takes to keep the momentum going. The important thing is to build a positive association with homework time, turning it from a dreaded task into something more manageable and even, dare we say it, enjoyable.

Organizational skills might seem like a far-off dream, but they're entirely achievable. Consider introducing colorful planners or digital tools that can help keep track of assignments, tests, and projects. Developing these skills doesn't just help in school; it's a valuable life skill. Work with your child to set up a system for organizing their materials - color-coded folders for different subjects, clear labels, and designated spaces for school supplies can help keep things in order. But remember, it's not about achieving perfection. It's about creating a system that works for them and makes it easier to find things they need.

Join forces with other parents. Having a support network can provide additional ideas and strategies. Sometimes, just hearing about another child's success with a particular approach can inspire you to try something new. Schools often have parent-teacher organizations, and attending these can also help build a support network.

Let's talk about communication. Regularly check in with your child about how they're feeling about school. Their feedback is invaluable. Encourage them to express any frustrations or challenges they face, and be their advocate. Addressing issues early can prevent them from escalating into larger problems. It's also an excellent way to teach them self-advocacy skills, encouraging them to speak up for their needs respectfully and effectively.

In all of these efforts, a sense of humor can be your best friend. When things don't go perfectly—and inevitably, they won't—laugh it off and try again. Academic success isn't just about grades; it's about fostering a love for learning and building resilience. Celebrate small victories and remind your child that every step forward, no matter how small, is progress.

Nothing beats seeing your child unlocked academic potential, watching them move from struggle to success right before your eyes. It's a team effort, and with the right strategies, your child can—and will—shine. Here's to supporting that journey!

Working with Educators

It's no secret that kids spend a significant part of their day at school. Therefore, collaborating with educators becomes an essential aspect of supporting your child's academic success. Teachers and school staff play crucial roles in your child's learning experiences, so building a strong partnership can make all the difference. In this section, we'll explore strategies for working effectively with educators to support your child with ADHD.

First and foremost, it's important to approach this collaboration with a mindset of teamwork and open communication. Teachers are on the front lines and often have valuable insights into your child's behavior and academic performance. When you show a genuine interest in their perspective, you create a foundation of mutual respect. Start by scheduling regular meetings with your child's teachers. These don't have to be lengthy; even a 15-minute chat can provide essential updates and align your efforts at home and school.

Next, make sure to share relevant information about your child upfront. If your child has an Individualized Education Plan (IEP) or a 504 Plan, ensure that it's shared and discussed with the teacher early in the school year. These plans serve as blueprints for accommodating your child's unique needs. It's also a good idea to provide a brief summary of your child's strengths and challenges, helping teachers understand how best to support them in the classroom.

One effective strategy is to create a home-school communication log. This can be a simple notebook or an online document where both you and the teacher can jot down notes about your child's progress, any issues that arise, or any strategies that seem to be working well. This ongoing dialogue keeps everyone in the loop and provides a written record that can be referred back to, ensuring that nothing falls through the cracks.

Teachers are more likely to respond positively if you approach them as partners rather than critics. Recognize the constraints they operate under —large class sizes, limited resources, and diverse student needs can make their job challenging. When discussing concerns, aim for constructive feedback and be open to brainstorming solutions together. Instead of saying, "You're not helping my child enough," try framing it as, "I noticed my child struggles with this. Could we explore some strategies that might work better?"

Additionally, familiarize yourself with the school's policies and resources. Many schools have specialized staff such as school counselors, occupational therapists, or special education teachers who can offer additional support. Knowing what resources are available can help you advocate more effectively for your child. Don't hesitate to request meetings with these specialists if you think they could provide valuable assistance. Often, these experts have a wealth of experience and can suggest interventions you might not have considered.

Moreover, consider volunteering or getting involved in school activities, if your schedule allows. Being present in the school community not only shows your commitment but also gives you a better understanding of the environment your child is navigating. It can provide opportunities for informal conversations with teachers and staff, further strengthening your collaborative relationship.

Empathy is another crucial element. Everyone involved wants the best for your child, but perspectives may differ. Offering understanding and patience goes a long way. If a teacher reports a challenging day, acknowledge their effort and stress the importance of ongoing collaboration. "I appreciate you letting me know. Let's keep working together to find what helps my child thrive" conveys partnership and shared goals.

Educators often appreciate specific, actionable suggestions rather than broad requests. For instance, if you know that your child benefits from visual aids or needs movement breaks, suggest these strategies tactfully. "I've noticed that visual schedules help my child stay focused. Could we try incorporating those in the classroom?" Specific recommendations are more actionable and can be seamlessly integrated into the classroom routine.

Another key aspect of working with educators is being proactive about problems before they escalate. If you notice early signs of struggle, address them with the teacher promptly. Waiting until parent-teacher conferences could mean losing valuable time that could have been used to implement effective strategies. Early intervention often translates to more manageable challenges and better outcomes for your child.

Understanding the school's assessment and grading system is also vital. If your child has accommodations, ensure they are being met consistently. Sometimes, new teachers may not be fully aware of the specific needs outlined in an IEP or 504 Plan. Regularly check in to make sure that accommodations like extended test time or additional breaks are being honored.

Balancing praise with concerns when communicating with educators can also be effective. Acknowledging what is working well builds goodwill and makes conversations about challenges less confrontational. Simple statements like, "My child really enjoys your math lessons and seems to respond well to your teaching style," can be very encouraging to teachers.

While focusing on academics is crucial, don't overlook social and emotional aspects. Discussing these with educators helps provide a holistic support system for your child. "I've noticed that my child has trouble making friends. Are there opportunities for guided social interactions during class?" This sort of dialogue ensures that both academic and socio-emotional needs are being addressed.

One of the overlooked benefits of a strong home-school partnership is the positive message it sends to your child. When children see their parents and teachers working together, they understand that they are supported by a united team. This sense of unity can significantly boost their confidence and willingness to put effort into their schoolwork.

Lastly, don't underestimate the power of gratitude. A simple thank-you note or a word of appreciation goes a long way. Teachers often hear more complaints than compliments, and recognizing their hard work can make them even more willing to go the extra mile for your child.

To wrap up, working effectively with educators involves ongoing communication, mutual respect, and a proactive approach. By sharing relevant information, offering constructive feedback, and showing empathy, you can build a strong, collaborative relationship that supports your child's academic success. Remember, the goal is to create a learning environment where your child feels understood, supported, and empowered to achieve their best.

Homework Help

Homework. It's the word that makes both parents and kids shudder, but it's an unavoidable part of academic life. For children with ADHD, homework can seem like climbing a mountain — sweaty, exhausting, and seemingly endless. But don't despair! There are effective strategies that can make this daily task more manageable. With the right tools and a bit of patience, you can transform homework time from a chaotic struggle into a smoother, more productive routine.

First and foremost, creating a dedicated homework space can do wonders. This space should be free from distractions like TVs, video games, or noisy siblings. A quiet, well-lit area with all necessary supplies at hand can create a conducive environment for focus. Remember, consistency is key. The brain loves patterns, especially for children with ADHD, so doing homework in the same place at the same time each day can help build a routine that fosters concentration and productivity.

Another helpful strategy is breaking down assignments into smaller, more manageable chunks. A page full of math problems might seem overwhelming, but tackling them in smaller groups can make the task feel less daunting. Use a timer to create short, focused work periods (sometimes called the Pomodoro Technique), followed by brief breaks. For example, 20 minutes of focused work followed by a 5-minute break can help maintain sustained attention and reduce burnout.

Also, it's crucial to prioritize tasks based on difficulty and deadline. Encouraging your child to start with the most challenging homework first can make the rest of the evening flow more smoothly. Besides, it's often easier to tackle difficult assignments when their energy levels are higher. Plus, finishing the toughest tasks upfront can provide a sense of accomplishment that motivates them to complete the rest.

Sometimes, the biggest hurdle is just getting started. This is where a "homework contract" can come in handy. A homework contract is an agreement between you and your child outlining expectations, timeframes, and rewards for completing homework. It helps to set clear guidelines and motivates your kiddo through positive reinforcement. Remember, the aim is to build good habits and a sense of accountability, not to add pressure.

Speaking of incentives, they can be powerful motivators if used wisely. While it may not seem ideal to reward kids for doing what they should be doing anyway, for children with ADHD, immediate reinforcements can work magic. Small rewards like extra screen time, a favorite snack, or a fun activity after completing homework can provide the motivation needed to stay on task.

If your child is struggling with a particular subject, consider seeking additional support. Tutors, homework clubs, or online resources can offer targeted help that might make a significant difference. Sometimes, a different perspective or a unique teaching style can make a concept click. Again, don't hesitate to collaborate with your child's teacher. They can offer insights and additional strategies tailored to your child's unique learning needs.

Another often overlooked tool is technology. Educational apps and tools designed for children with ADHD can turn homework into a more interactive and engaging experience. Apps like Khan Academy, Grammarly, or even using voice-to-text features can help kids who struggle with traditional methods. Just ensure that screen time is balanced and focused on educational content to avoid any slippery distractions.

Organization can be another critical area where kids with ADHD may need assistance. Help them use planners or digital tools to track assignments and deadlines. Visual aids like color-coded folders, checklists, or whiteboards can make a big difference. Every child is different, so it might take some experimentation to find out what organizational system works best for them. Small, gradual adjustments can eventually lead to significant improvements.

It's also important to foster a growth mindset. Praising effort rather than the outcome can help build resilience and a willingness to tackle challenging tasks. Statements like "I'm proud of how hard you worked on that project" rather than "You did such a good job" shift the focus to the effort, which can be more encouraging in the long run.

This approach cultivates a habit of perseverance and a healthy attitude towards learning and challenges.

As engaging as these strategies are, it's essential to recognize and accommodate for mental and physical fatigue. Kids with ADHD may have shorter attention spans and tire more quickly after school. Allow them to decompress before diving into homework. After all, a relaxed mind is more ready to learn. Snack breaks, a short exercise session, or simply some quiet time can reset their focus and make homework less of a struggle.

Sometimes, the best way to help is simply by being there. Sit with them during homework time. Your presence can provide reassurance and can help keep them on track. Supervision doesn't mean micromanaging but being available to guide and clarify where needed. Just be careful not to do the work for them; the goal is to support independence and confidence in their abilities.

Lastly, maintaining open lines of communication is crucial. Frequently check in with your child to see how they're feeling about their homework. If they're overwhelmed or frustrated, this can be an opportunity to troubleshoot and adjust strategies accordingly. Listening actively can make your child feel supported and understood, which is half the battle in managing ADHD-related homework challenges.

In summary, homework help for children with ADHD is about creating a supportive, structured, and flexible environment that accommodates their unique needs. With the right strategies in place, you can turn homework from a battle into a more manageable part of your daily routine. Stay positive, stay patient, and remember — every step forward, no matter how small, is a success worth celebrating. Happy studying!

Organizational Skills

So, you've got a child with ADHD and you're looking for ways to support their academic success. One crucial skill that often gets overlooked but can make a world of difference is organizational ability. Let's face it, organization can be challenging for anyone, but for kids with ADHD, it's often an even bigger mountain to climb. With the right strategies and tools, though, it can absolutely be done.

First off, let's talk about the physical environment. A cluttered desk or a messy room can be incredibly distracting. For a child with ADHD, it can feel like trying to find a single drop of water in the ocean. Start small. Have designated spots for everything—books, supplies, electronics. It's not just about cleanliness; it's about creating a space where distractions are minimized, and focus can flourish.

Parents can play an essential role in this aspect. Think of it as setting the stage for a play. The actors (your children) need a well-organized stage to deliver their best performance. Simple actions like spending an hour each weekend organizing and tidying up can set a strong foundation for the week ahead. Use bins, color-coded folders, and labels. It'll make finding things a breeze and teach your child the value of a well-organized space.

Another big piece of the organizational puzzle is time management. Let's be honest, mastering time is tough for anyone, and the challenge can be even greater for children with ADHD. Teaching them to break down tasks into manageable chunks can make assignments and chores less daunting. Use timers to create a sense of urgency and provide visual schedules to give a clear picture of what needs to be done and when.

One effective strategy is the "15-minute rule." Give your child a task and set a timer for 15 minutes. This helps to create a deadline and adds a bit of gamification to the process. They work on the task for 15 minutes, and then they get a break or a small reward. This can help build focus and make completing tasks less overwhelming.

Calendars and planners aren't just for adults. Your child can benefit enormously from having a personal planner. Whether it's a small notebook they can carry to school or an app on their device, the act of writing down assignments and important dates can help improve their memory and organizational skills. Teach them to use different colors for different subjects or activities. Visual cues can be incredibly powerful.

Let's not forget the role of technology. Numerous apps and tools are designed to aid in organization. From to-do lists to scheduling apps, there are tons of resources to explore. Just make sure the technology works as a tool and doesn't become another distraction. Apps like Trello or Todoist can be particularly useful for managing tasks and setting reminders.

Parental involvement is crucial. Check in regularly. But, here's a secret: try to make these check-ins collaborative rather than authoritative. Ask questions like "What do you think you need to do next?" or "How do you feel about your progress?" This can help children feel more in control and more invested in staying organized.

One indispensable tool for maintaining organization is the humble checklist. Encourage your child to create a list every morning or every evening for the next day. This could include school assignments, chores, or any other tasks. Checking off completed items can give a sense of accomplishment and serve as a visual representation of their progress.

Don't underestimate the power of routine, either. Consistency is a key ally in the battle against disorganization. Establishing regular times for homework, chores, and even relaxation can create a structured environment that helps your child know what to expect. Predictability can be very comforting and reduce anxiety.

Of course, it's essential to adapt and adjust. No system is one-size-fits-all. What works for one child might not work for another. Keep tweaking and refining your approach based on what you're observing. Empower your child to have a say in how things are organized—it'll make them feel more involved and less like they're being micromanaged.

Incorporate some fun elements. Use sticker charts or small rewards to reinforce good organization habits. A bit of positive reinforcement can go a long way in making these skills stick.

Remember, the goal isn't perfection. The aim is progress. Celebrate small victories and be patient with setbacks. Organizational skills, like any other skill, take time to develop and hone. With persistence and creativity, your child can certainly master them and, in turn, find more academic success.

The journey towards organizational mastery may be long and winding, but with each step, you're helping your child build skills that will serve them well throughout their lives. Balance structure with flexibility, guidance with independence, and you'll be on the right path. Happy organizing!

Chapter 7:
Encouraging Social Skills

So you've tackled the basics of understanding ADHD, built a solid relationship with your child, and even created an effective routine. Now comes a critical part of your journey: encouraging social skills. For children with ADHD, social interactions can be particularly challenging. They may struggle with reading social cues or displaying empathy, making it hard for them to form and maintain friendships. But fret not; there are practical ways to help them navigate these social waters.

First off, let's dive into empathy. Teaching empathy starts at home. Children learn by watching, and they often look to their parents as role models. Make it a habit to verbalize your thoughts when you notice someone else's feelings. For example, you might say, "I see that Sarah is upset because her toy broke. How do you think we could help her feel better?" This lets your child understand and value others' emotions.

And let's be honest: developing empathy is a gradual process. It won't happen overnight. You can help speed things up by reading books that focus on emotional intelligence or watching shows that emphasize understanding others. Use these as conversation starters to explore what the characters might be feeling and why.

Role-playing scenarios can be a lifesaver here. Kids love playing pretend, and it can be a fun way to practice social situations. Use role-playing to run through different social scenarios your child may encounter, such as greeting a new friend, sharing toys, or dealing with a disagreement. Practice how to introduce themselves, make eye contact, and even how to exit a conversation gracefully.

Remember, practice makes perfect, but positive reinforcement makes it stick. Whenever your child shows social awareness or does something kind, acknowledge it. Saying, "I noticed how nicely you shared your toy with your friend today," reinforces good behavior more effectively than reprimanding mistakes.

Another focus should be on social activities that promote inclusion. Sports teams, clubs, and group classes can offer structured environments for your child to practice social skills. For kids who shy away from large groups, smaller, more supervised settings might work better. The goal here isn't to overwhelm them but to gradually build their confidence in social settings.

Be mindful of what activities your child is naturally drawn to. Some children with ADHD may thrive in physical activities like soccer or dance, while others may prefer more creative outlets like art classes or drama clubs. Observe what brings your child joy and seek out group activities in those areas.

Don't underestimate the power of unstructured playdates, either. Inviting one or two friends over for a playdate can create a low-pressure environment where your child can practice social interactions. Keep these playdates short initially and gradually extend them as your child becomes more comfortable.

If your child struggles with certain behaviors during social interactions, such as interrupting or being too impulsive, having a quiet and private discussion about these incidents later can be beneficial. Use these moments as teaching opportunities, offering gentle advice on how to handle similar situations differently in the future.

Encouraging social skills also means understanding your child's unique challenges. They might feel overwhelmed in large crowds or noisy environments. Always be prepared with coping strategies, such as finding a quiet space for breaks, having a comforting object on hand, or practicing deep-breathing techniques together.

Lastly, collaboration with teachers and school counselors can be incredibly valuable. Teachers can give you insights into how your child interacts with peers in a different setting, which can be useful information to tailor your home strategies.

Navigating social skills with a child who has ADHD can feel like you're embarking on a long journey without a map. But step by step, with empathy, practice, and positive reinforcement, your child will gain the social skills they need to create meaningful and lasting friendships. Keep fostering these skills with patience and love, and you'll be amazed at the progress they can make.

Teaching Empathy

Teaching empathy is a critical component in encouraging social skills, particularly for children with ADHD. Empathy, the ability to understand and share the feelings of another, can be a powerful tool in enhancing social interactions. It's not just about identifying emotions in others but also understanding the why behind those emotions. For children with ADHD, this can be a bit of a challenge due to their impulsivity and focus issues, but with the right guidance, they can develop strong empathetic abilities.

One effective method for teaching empathy is through storytelling. Stories have a unique way of drawing us into the lives and emotions of others. When you read a story to your child, pause at moments of conflict or emotional intensity. Ask questions like, "How do you think this character feels?" or "Why might they be feeling that way?" This simple exercise encourages your child to step into someone else's shoes and consider different perspectives.

Another practical approach is through real-life examples. If your child comes home upset because a friend didn't share a toy, use that moment as a teaching tool. You might say, "It sounds like your friend was feeling pretty protective of that toy. How do you feel when you're really excited about something and someone else wants to use it?" This helps your child relate personally to others' emotions and understand that their feelings aren't unique; others feel similarly in different situations.

Modeling empathy in your day-to-day interactions can also have a profound impact. Children learn a great deal from observing the behavior of adults around them. Express understanding and compassion in your interactions with others. For example, if a cashier seems upset, you might say, "It looks like you're having a rough day. I hope things get better soon." Your child observes these actions and learns to replicate them.

Empathy can also be fostered through role-playing scenarios. This not only builds empathy but also prepares children for different social situations. For instance, you could role-play a situation where a friend is left out of a game. Your child can practice what they might say or do to include the friend, experiencing both perspectives during the role-play. This can make real-life situations less intimidating and more manageable.

Inclusion in social activities can be another significant stepping stone. Allow and encourage your child to partake in group activities, whether it's a sports team, a music group, or a club. These settings provide ample opportunities for your child to practice empathy by interacting with a diverse set of peers. The dynamics of group activities naturally create moments where empathy is required, helping your child build and refine this essential skill.

Open communication in the family setting is also crucial. Make time for regular family discussions where everyone can share their feelings and experiences. This practice not only strengthens family bonds but also demonstrates that it's safe and valuable to express emotions. Use these discussions to explore and validate each other's feelings, showing your child that empathy is a core family value.

Humor and light-heartedness can play a role here too. Sometimes situations require a gentle touch, a shared laugh, to lighten the mood and make the lessons more memorable. For example, if your child forgets to think before acting and feels bad afterward, keep it light. Share a funny story from your own childhood where you did something similar. It reassures your child that everyone makes mistakes and feeling empathy towards themselves is important too.

Lastly, it's important to note that building empathy is a gradual process. Don't expect overnight success. Celebrate small victories and gently guide your child through setbacks. When they show empathy, acknowledge it and praise their effort. Positive reinforcement can go a long way in making empathetic behavior a natural part of your child's interactions.

In conclusion, teaching empathy is an ongoing journey filled with stories, real-life examples, role-playing, and inclusion. By consistently modeling empathetic behavior and fostering open communication within your family, your child will gradually develop the ability to understand and share the feelings of others. This foundational social skill not only aids in their immediate social interactions but sets the stage for meaningful, compassionate relationships throughout their life.

Role-Playing Scenarios

Let's dive into role-playing scenarios! Imagine this as a practice session for social interactions, where the stage is set, and everyone gets to be a star.

Role-playing can be an incredibly powerful tool for teaching children social skills. It allows them to step into someone else's shoes and view situations from different perspectives. This exercise is particularly beneficial for kids with ADHD, as it offers a structured environment to practice new behaviors and responses. Plus, it can be a lot of fun!

Firstly, start by identifying the social situation you're going to role-play. Is it making a new friend at the playground? Handling a disagreement? Asking for help from a teacher? Once you've chosen a scenario, it's time to assign roles. You can play the friend, the teacher, or another character, while the child plays themselves. You may also switch roles to let the child understand different viewpoints.

When setting up a scenario, ensure it's simple and specific. For example, if the scenario is about making a new friend, you can say, "You're at the park, and you see a kid playing with a toy you like. What do you do?" Guide them through possible responses, demonstrating and discussing the good, better, and best ways to act. Encourage the child to think aloud and explain their choices.

The key to successful role-playing is repetition and gradual complexity. Start with easy scenarios, and as the child gains confidence, introduce more complex situations. Practice the same scenario multiple times if needed, so the child becomes comfortable with the responses. Consistency is crucial for helping them internalize these skills.

Don't forget the importance of positive reinforcement. Praise your child for their effort, creativity, and any correct responses they give. If they struggle, use it as a teaching moment. Rather than saying, "That's wrong," you can ask, "How else could we handle this?" or provide gentle guidance to steer them toward more appropriate responses.

Another effective approach is to use real-life situations as role-playing opportunities. For instance, if you notice your child having difficulty waiting their turn, you can reenact the scenario at home and practice the right behavior. This strategy helps bridge the gap between the practice environment and real-world application.

It's also beneficial to involve siblings or friends in role-playing activities. This dynamic provides a more authentic experience and helps children with ADHD learn to navigate group interactions. Plus, it fosters a collaborative and supportive atmosphere at home.

Additionally, using props and costumes can make role-playing more engaging. If your child is reluctant or shy, incorporating their favorite toys or dressing up can turn the activity into an exciting game. Remember, the goal is to make learning social skills enjoyable and stress-free.

Let's consider a few more detailed scenarios:

- **Handling a Bully:** A common concern for many parents. Role-play different strategies like seeking help from an adult, using assertive language, or walking away. Discuss the pros and cons of each strategy.

- **Joining a Group Activity:** Many kids with ADHD find it tough to integrate into group activities. Practice phrases and approaches they can use, like asking, "Can I join in?" or observing and then participating when there's an opening.

- **Expressing Feelings:** It's challenging for children with ADHD to articulate their emotions. Role-play situations where they might need to express anger, disappointment, or joy. Teach them phrases such as, "I feel upset because..."

Parents, don't hesitate to take on different emotional responses during these role-plays. Show your child what positive and negative reactions from others might look like, so they can learn to adjust their behavior accordingly. It's also a helpful way to teach empathy, by showing how their actions affect others.

For situations that occur frequently, create scripts. If your child struggles with asking peers to play, writing a simple script they can memorize might be useful. It could go something like, "Hi, my name is

[Name]. Can I play with you?" Over time, as they get comfortable with the script, they can start to improvise naturally.

Incorporating humor can also enhance role-playing scenarios. Kids love to laugh, and making these sessions lighthearted can reduce anxiety and resistance. Use silly voices, exaggerated expressions, or playful scenarios. The more they enjoy the activity, the more engaged they will be.

Remember, patience is your ally throughout this process. Children with ADHD often need more time to adjust to new skills and behaviors. Celebrate small victories, and maintain a positive, encouraging atmosphere. Your consistent effort in these role-playing sessions will pay off, leading to improved social interactions for your child.

Finally, stay consistent but flexible. Schedule regular role-playing practice, maybe three times a week. But if a spontaneous teaching moment arises, don't hesitate to seize it. Blend structured sessions with organic opportunities to create a balanced learning environment.

Role-playing scenarios aren't just about teaching social skills. They are about fostering empathy, improving communication, and building confidence in navigating social interactions. So, transform your living room into a stage, put on your imaginative hats, and let the learning through play begin!

Social Activities and Inclusion

Social activities play a crucial role in encouraging social skills among children with ADHD. By participating in various group events or activities, they get the chance to practice and improve their social interactions in real-world settings. These experiences provide invaluable opportunities to learn how to share, take turns, collaborate, and resolve conflicts with peers.

Engaging in team sports can be an especially effective way for children with ADHD to build their social skills. Sports like soccer, basketball, or even cooperative games teach kids about teamwork, communication, and the value of working together to achieve common goals. Plus, the physical activity itself can help in channeling their energy and improving focus. However, it's important to choose activities that align with your child's interests and strengths.

Art classes, music groups, and drama clubs are also fantastic outlets. These activities allow children to express themselves creatively while learning to work with others. Art and music, in particular, can serve as non-verbal means of communication, giving children a way to connect with peers without the pressure of extensive talking.

Another valuable option is joining clubs or organizations that cater to specific interests, such as scouting groups or coding clubs. These settings allow kids to meet others who share their passions, making it easier to connect and form friendships. Moreover, these clubs often have structured activities and clear rules, which can be beneficial for children who struggle with less structured environments.

It's worth mentioning the significance of inclusive education and play. Schools and community centers that embrace inclusive practices create a supportive environment where children with ADHD feel valued and understood. These inclusive settings not only help children with ADHD develop socially but also promote understanding and empathy among all students.

Don't overlook the importance of family activities, either. Family game nights, outings, and even regular family dinners can be excellent opportunities for practicing social skills in a safe and loving environment. During these times, you can model appropriate social behaviors and gently guide your child in navigating social interactions.

It's essential to prepare your child for social activities by discussing what to expect and role-playing potential scenarios. For instance, before a playdate, you might practice how to greet friends, share toys, and ask to join in games. This preparation can boost your child's confidence and reduce anxiety about social situations.

Remember that not all social interactions will go smoothly, and that's okay. Mistakes and misunderstandings are part of the learning process. Use these moments as teaching opportunities to discuss what happened and how different choices might lead to better outcomes in the future. Encourage your child to reflect on their experiences and think about what they can do differently next time.

Including children with ADHD in mainstream activities is crucial, but sometimes they may benefit from the support of specialized programs. Social skills groups or therapy sessions led by professionals can provide targeted support and a safe space for children to practice and develop their social abilities under the guidance of experts.

One must also consider the role of technology in social inclusion. Online games and virtual group activities can provide additional avenues for social engagement, especially for children who may feel overwhelmed in face-to-face settings. However, it's essential to monitor and guide their online interactions to ensure they are positive and safe.

Volunteering together as a family can be another excellent way to foster social skills and a sense of community. Activities like participating in community clean-ups or helping at a local food bank allow children to interact with various people and develop a sense of empathy and responsibility toward others.

Helping your child develop social skills is an ongoing process that involves patience, persistence, and plenty of practice. Celebrate their social successes, no matter how small, and provide lots of positive reinforcement. Social skills don't develop overnight, but with consistent support and encouragement, your child can build the confidence and competence they need to navigate social situations successfully.

Ultimately, the goal is to help children with ADHD feel included and connected to their peers. By providing them with ample opportunities to engage in social activities, preparing them for those situations, and supporting them through the ups and downs, you are setting them up for social success and helping them build meaningful, lasting relationships.

Chapter 8:
Boosting Self-Esteem

Self-esteem is the fuel that propels us through life. For children with ADHD, cultivating strong self-worth is essential but often challenging. The unique hurdles they face can chip away at their confidence, making it vital to focus on boosting self-esteem consistently.

Celebrating Strengths

Every child has their own set of strengths, and highlighting these can do wonders for their self-image. This isn't about empty praise — it's about genuine recognition of their talents and achievements. Whether it's artistic ability, a knack for solving puzzles, or being a good friend, acknowledging these areas helps children see themselves in a positive light.

Consistently celebrating strengths creates a positive feedback loop. When children feel good about their abilities, they're more likely to take on challenges and show resilience in the face of setbacks. Keep an eye out for progress, no matter how small, and make a big deal out of it. A simple, "I saw how hard you worked on that project; you're really improving!" can mean the world to them.

Building Confidence

Confidence doesn't just appear out of thin air; it's built through experience and encouragement. Encourage your child to take small, manageable risks that can lead to success. These mini-challenges can build up their confidence incrementally. Trying new activities, whether it's a sport, music, or even cooking, adds to their repertoire of successes.

If they're naturally apprehensive, start small. Remember, the goal is to create opportunities for success. Even activities like organizing their room or helping with a household task can be structured for achievement. The satisfaction they derive from completing a task builds confidence.

Positive Self-Talk

How children talk to themselves plays a critical role in their self-esteem. Negative self-talk can be particularly detrimental for kids with ADHD. They might say things like, "I'm stupid" or "I can't do anything right." These thoughts need to be countered with positive affirmations.

Teaching positive self-talk involves modeling it yourself. When you praise them, use specific, positive words. Encourage them to repeat affirmations such as, "I am capable," or "I can figure this out." If they make a mistake, frame it as a learning experience rather than a failure.

Sometimes, visual aids like sticky notes with positive messages can serve as gentle reminders. Place these notes in their study area or on the bathroom mirror. Simple affirmations can gradually rewire the negative narrative they've developed over time.

Boosting self-esteem in children with ADHD isn't a one-time event; it's an ongoing process. Celebrate their strengths consistently, help them build confidence through small successes, and foster a positive internal dialogue. With patience and persistent effort, you'll give them the tools they need to see their own worth, setting the foundation for a more confident future.

Celebrating Strengths

One of the most powerful ways to boost self-esteem in children with ADHD is by celebrating their unique strengths. This approach shifts the focus from challenges and weaknesses to the child's innate talents and capabilities, offering a more balanced and positive perspective. Recognizing and celebrating strengths is more than just a feel-good exercise; it's a vital strategy for helping children build confidence and resilience.

Imagine a child who consistently struggles with attention in class but excels at creative writing or art. Instead of solely focusing on the difficulties with attention, acknowledging and celebrating the child's artistic talents can offer them a much-needed confidence boost. These strengths are not only areas where the child can shine but can also serve as a foundation for leveraging weaker skills.

One of the most effective ways to start celebrating strengths is by creating a "Strengths Chart" at home. This can be a simple poster board where everyone in the family writes down the specific strengths they observe in the child. This visual representation serves as a constant reminder of their capabilities and achievements, which can be incredibly uplifting. Periodically reviewing and adding to the chart ensures that the child's evolving talents are recognized and applauded.

Another method is through storytelling. Share stories, either from your own experiences or from famous individuals who have turned their unique skills into their greatest assets. For instance, did you know that many successful entrepreneurs have ADHD? Stories of resilience and triumph can inspire children to see their strengths as pivotal components of their future successes.

- Include stories about athletes who harnessed their high energy levels to excel in sports.

- Talk about creative geniuses who used their endless imagination to innovate and create.

- Discuss business leaders who turned their out-of-the-box thinking into disruptive solutions.

Similarly, enrolling your child in activities where they naturally excel can also help in reinforcing their strengths. Whether it's a sports team, a music class, or an art workshop, these environments provide opportunities for them to not only employ their skills but also to receive positive feedback. The sense of accomplishment from these activities can significantly boost their overall self-esteem.

Regularly practice strength-based language. Instead of saying, "You did well in spite of your ADHD," say, "Your creativity really shows in this drawing." The former implies that ADHD is a barrier, while the latter emphasizes the child's talent. This shift in language can have a profound impact on how children perceive themselves and their abilities.

Moreover, it's important to celebrate not just the big wins but also the small, everyday achievements. Did your child complete their homework without being reminded? That's worth celebrating! Did they help out a sibling or friend? Another win! These smaller, frequent celebrations add up over time and gradually build a stronger, more positive self-image.

A fun way to mark small achievements is by using a "Success Jar." Place a jar in a common area of your home and every time your child achieves something, no matter how small, write it on a slip of paper and drop it in the jar. On particularly tough days, reviewing the contents of the success jar can be a great morale booster.

Additionally, encourage self-reflection. Teach your child to recognize their own strengths by asking questions like, "What are you proud of today?" or "What was something you did well this week?" This practice not only helps in identifying strengths but also develops a habit of focusing on the positive aspects of their day-to-day experiences.

Engage with teachers and caregivers to reinforce this approach. Often, educators focus on academic or behavioral challenges, but keeping them in the loop about celebrating strengths can promote a more balanced perspective at school as well. Regular communication between parents and teachers can ensure that strengths are acknowledged in both home and school environments.

Lastly, leverage the power of positive self-talk. Encourage your child to use affirmations and remind them of their strengths. This can be something as simple as saying, "I am a good friend," or "I am creative." These affirmations help to internalize a positive self-view and can serve as a counterbalance to the negative self-talk that children with ADHD might engage in.

Incorporating these strategies into your daily routine doesn't require sweeping changes or significant effort. Simple, consistent actions can establish a strong foundation of self-esteem that will support your child throughout their life. Celebrating strengths is not only about boosting self-esteem; it's about fostering a lifelong appreciation for one's unique capabilities and the positive impact they can have on the world.

As we embrace the practice of celebrating strengths, remember that every child is a blend of challenges and remarkable talents. By consciously choosing to highlight and celebrate these talents, we help our children see themselves through a lens of potential rather than deficiency. In the next section, we'll explore ways to build confidence further through deliberate and supportive practices. Keep this momentum going—you're doing amazing work!

Building Confidence

Confidence is like a muscle; it needs regular exercise to grow strong. Especially for children with ADHD, building confidence can sometimes seem like a Herculean task, but it's far from impossible. It does, however, require persistence, patience, and a sprinkling of creativity.

When it comes to boosting your child's self-esteem, the first step is to focus on their strengths. Everyone has something they're good at, and kids with ADHD are no exception. Maybe they're great at drawing, perhaps they're natural athletes, or maybe they have a knack for making people laugh. Whatever their strength is, highlight it. Celebrate it. Let them know how special and unique it makes them. By shining a spotlight on their strengths, you are laying a solid foundation for their confidence to build upon.

Now, it's important to acknowledge that kids with ADHD often hear a lot more about what they're doing wrong than what they're doing right. Negative feedback can be overwhelming and detrimental to their self- esteem. Instead, make it a point to offer genuine praise for their efforts as often as possible. And remember, it's not just about praising the outcome but the effort that went into it. When your child struggles with a math problem but gives it their best shot, that's worth recognizing.

Consistency in routines and expectations can also play a significant role in building confidence. Kids thrive when they know what's coming next and what's expected of them. If every morning starts with a structured routine where tasks are clearly laid out, children with ADHD can mentally prepare for each step. Navigate morning routines with task charts, timers, and visual aids, making the process smoother and reducing anxiety. This kind of predictable environment can make them feel more secure and capable, giving their confidence a much-needed boost.

Dealing with failures or setbacks is another critical aspect of confidence- building. Teaching your child that it's okay to fail and more importantly, how to bounce back from failure, can be transformative. Engage in conversations about famous personalities who faced numerous failures before achieving success. Encourage a growth mindset by emphasizing that failure is not the end but simply a stepping stone. Provide practical examples from their daily life to illustrate how each setback is an opportunity to learn and grow.

Including your child in decision-making processes can also work wonders. Let them have a say in choosing weekend activities or even picking out their clothes for the day. This empowerment helps them realize that their opinions matter and they have control over certain aspects of their lives. When they see that their choices lead to positive outcomes, their confidence naturally blossoms.

It's also beneficial to set achievable goals and encourage your child to strive towards them. Breaking down larger tasks into smaller, manageable steps can make even the most daunting challenges seem surmountable. Celebrate every small victory along the way to reinforce their belief in their abilities. Remember, it's about the journey as much as it's about the destination.

Of course, youthful energy is boundless, and channeling that energy positively can greatly influence a child's self-esteem. Physical activities, team sports, or any group activities can offer excellent avenues for them to shine. Not only do these practices keep them physically fit, but they also instill a sense of camaraderie and accomplishment.

Role-modeling is another powerful tool in your toolkit. Demonstrate self- confidence in your actions and words because kids are quick to mirror the behavior of adults they look up to. Show how you tackle challenging tasks and deal with your failures with grace. When they observe how you handle life's ups and downs, they'll learn to apply similar strategies in their own lives.

Finally, emphasize the importance of self-talk. Encourage them to replace negative thoughts with positive affirmations like "I can do this" or "I am capable." You might create a daily ritual where you both share one thing you like about yourselves. It might feel a bit awkward at first, but over time, positive self-talk can become second nature, bolstering their internal confidence.

Building confidence is an ongoing process, and there'll be bumps along the way. But with targeted efforts and unwavering support, children with ADHD can develop the self-assurance they need to thrive. Every small win, every hurdle overcome, contributes to a stronger, more confident individual. And remember, the fruits of your labor will not only be evident in childhood but will resonate throughout their entire lives. So, let's get to work, and enjoy the journey of fostering confidence in your child.

Positive Self-Talk

Let's dive into the realm of positive self-talk and its monumental role in boosting self-esteem for children with ADHD. Imagine self-talk as the running commentary in your mind. It's what you tell yourself throughout the day about your experiences and actions. For children with ADHD, this self-talk can sometimes be overwhelmingly negative, filled with doubts and self-criticism. That's why fostering positive self-talk is crucial. It's about teaching them to be their own cheerleaders, turning self-criticism into encouragement.

First off, let's acknowledge that achieving positive self-talk isn't an overnight transformation. It's a gradual process. But the good news is that even small steps can make a significant difference. Children with ADHD often compare themselves unfavorably to their peers, which can erode their self-esteem. By guiding them to focus on their strengths rather than their perceived weaknesses, we can slowly rebuild their confidence. A simple but powerful phrase like "I can do this" can gradually replace "I always mess up."

One practical approach is to create a "positivity journal." Encourage your child to jot down at least one positive thought or accomplishment each day. Did they finish their homework on time? Did they help a friend? Writing these moments down reinforces the idea that they are capable and valued. Plus, this journal can be a go-to resource for them to revisit whenever they're feeling down.

Another useful method is role-playing. Role-playing scenarios where children practice positive self-talk can help them internalize this mindset. For example, if a child is nervous about an upcoming test, act out the situation with them. Have them verbalize their fears first, and then guide them to counter those fears with positive statements like "I studied hard, and I know the material."

Now, let's talk about the influence of language. The words we use matter. Encouraging children to replace self-defeating phrases with empowering ones can transform their internal dialogue. Phrases like "I'm stupid" can be switched to "I made a mistake, but I can learn from it." Simple language changes can create a transformative ripple effect in how they perceive themselves.

Alongside this, it's important to model positive self-talk yourself. Children pick up on the behavior and language of the adults around them. When they see you handling your own challenges with positive self-talk, they learn to mimic that resilience. Saying things out loud like "I can figure this out" or "I'm doing my best" during your own tough times can be incredibly educational.

Adding humor to the mix can also lighten the atmosphere and make the lessons stick. For example, if your child is frustrated because they've forgotten something again, you might say, "Well, I guess we can add 'forgetting things' to our superhero skill list! What can we do to remember next time?" This not only diffuses the tension but also shows that mistakes are part of life and can be handled with a positive attitude.

Moreover, it's beneficial to surround children with positivity. Set up an environment in your home where uplifting words and affirmations are the norm. Stick positive notes where they can see them daily. Messages like "You are capable" or "Believe in yourself" can serve as constant, gentle reminders.

Now, let's not overlook the power of gratitude. Encouraging children to express gratitude can shift their focus from what's going wrong to what's going right. A "gratitude jar" can be a fun and engaging activity. Each day, have your child write down something they're grateful for and drop it into the jar. Over time, this collection of positive notes can be a wonderful resource for them to see how many good things exist in their lives.

Also, let's talk about mindfulness. Practicing mindfulness can help children become more aware of their thoughts and feelings. Simple mindfulness exercises, like deep breathing or short meditations, can help them pause and reflect before reacting negatively. Over time, mindfulness can cultivate a more balanced and positive internal dialogue.

Finally, recognize and celebrate progress frequently. Small victories are still victories and deserve recognition. Whether it's completing a task without prompting or handling a difficult situation calmly, these moments should be celebrated. Positive reinforcement helps to cement these behaviors, making positive self-talk a natural part of their routine.

In conclusion, fostering positive self-talk is an ongoing journey, but it's one that promises immense benefits for building self-esteem in children with ADHD. By making these practices a part of daily life, you'll help your child view themselves in a more positive and empowering light. It's not just about changing their words; it's about changing their world, one encouraging phrase at a time.

Chapter 9:
Managing Emotions

In the whirlwind of life with ADHD, emotions can sometimes feel like runaway trains. It's something many parents struggle with, wondering how best to help their children manage overwhelming feelings. This chapter dives into practical strategies for recognizing emotional triggers, implementing coping mechanisms, and adopting mindfulness practices that can make a world of difference.

Recognizing Triggers

Understanding what triggers emotional outbursts is like discovering hidden treasure. You can start by keeping a simple journal. Note down situations where your child seems particularly prone to meltdowns or excessive excitement. Is it during transitions, like leaving the house or finishing a favorite activity? Identifying patterns will give you valuable insights.

For instance, if your child loses their cool every time they have to stop playing video games, that's a critical clue. With that knowledge, you can set up a more gradual transition plan. Provide a ten-minute warning, followed by a five-minute reminder, and so on. This gradual easing can make the process less jarring.

Don't underestimate the power of sensory triggers either. Overstimulation from bright lights, loud noises, or even scratchy clothing can ramp up emotions. Creating a calm, predictable environment helps reduce these sensory triggers. Simple changes like using softer lighting or ensuring a cozy spot in the house can work wonders.

Coping Strategies

While it's crucial to recognize what sets off emotional reactions, equally important is equipping your child with effective coping skills. One technique is the "pause and breathe" approach. Teach your child to stop whatever they are doing and take deep, slow breaths. This might seem simplistic, but it helps activate the body's relaxation response.

An accessible strategy involves a "Feelings Chart." Create a chart with various emotions along with faces illustrating each emotion. Encourage your child to point to how they feel and discuss why they feel that way. This fosters emotional literacy and normalizes the experience of fluctuating emotions.

Another engaging tactic is "The Worry Box." If your child tends to ruminate on worries, provide a decorative box where they can "deposit" their worries written on slips of paper. Once the worry is in the box, it's no longer their immediate concern. This mental trick can be surprisingly effective.

Physical outlets for emotion are often needed too. Consider 'heavy work' activities like pushing a weighted cart, pulling a wagon, or even simple exercises like jumping jacks. These actions provide sensory feedback that can help regulate emotional states.

Mindfulness Practices

Mindfulness isn't just a buzzword; it's a powerful tool for managing emotions. Introducing these practices early can set the stage for life-long emotional resilience. Start with short, simple activities. Even a few minutes of focused breathing or a guided imagery session can help.

One popular method is the "5-4-3-2-1" grounding technique. Encourage your child to notice:

- 5 things they can see

- 4 things they can touch

- 3 things they can hear

- 2 things they can smell

- 1 thing they can taste

This exercise helps bring their focus to the present moment and away from overwhelming thoughts or feelings. Over time, they will start using this technique themselves when they feel an emotional storm brewing.

You might also explore mindful activities like "body scans," where your child closes their eyes and pays attention to different parts of their body, from their toes to their head. Guided meditations designed for children are widely available and can be a fun way to introduce these concepts.

Yoga can also be a valuable mindfulness practice. Basic yoga poses combined with deep breathing can help children attain a peaceful, focused state. You don't need specialized training to guide your child through some elementary poses; numerous child-friendly resources can help you get started.

Remember that consistency is key. Integrate these practices into your daily routine to make them second nature. Perhaps every evening, before bedtime, you dedicate ten minutes for a mindfulness exercise. The long- term benefits of these practices are profound. They can help your child not just in managing their emotions day-to-day but also in developing emotional intelligence as they grow older.

However, it's essential to maintain realistic expectations. Your child won't become a Zen master overnight. There will be setbacks, and that's perfectly okay. Celebrate small victories—like successfully using a breathing technique to calm down—and support your child through the tougher moments.

Managing emotions isn't something that happens in isolation. It's a skill developed over time, nurtured by a supportive environment. Be patient with your child and yourself. With the right strategies, emotional outbursts will become more manageable, leading to a calmer, more peaceful household. It's all about finding what methods resonate best with your child and making them part of your daily rhythm.

By taking the time to recognize triggers, implement coping strategies, and explore mindfulness practices, you'll be giving your child the tools they need not just to cope, but to thrive. It's a journey worth taking, one that promises a horizon where emotional balance is within reach.

Recognizing Triggers

Managing emotions in children with ADHD often starts with recognizing triggers. Knowing what sets off certain behaviors is crucial for crafting effective responses and fostering a supportive environment. Observing daily interactions and identifying patterns can be eye-opening. For instance, some children might become overwhelmed in noisy environments, whereas others could struggle more with sudden changes in routine.

One common trigger is sensory overload. Imagine your child walking into a brightly lit, crowded supermarket. The constant hum of neon lights, the chatter of shoppers, and the beeping of barcode scanners create a sensory maze that can lead to emotional outbursts. It's not just the volume of stimuli but their unpredictability that can be particularly overwhelming. Recognizing this, you can plan grocery runs during quieter times or, if possible, involve your child in a smaller list of items, making the trip more manageable.

Another prevalent trigger is transitions. Moving from one activity to another can be a significant challenge. If your child is deeply engrossed in a video game and you suddenly announce that it's time for dinner, you might see a meltdown. This isn't merely disobedience. It's a difficulty in shifting focus and adapting to a new task. What can help here is providing advance notices—five-minute warnings, for instance—so they can mentally prepare for the change. Visual timetables are also lifesavers, offering a clear outline of the day's schedule.

Social interactions can also serve as major triggers. For children who struggle with understanding social cues, playgrounds or group settings can quickly become overwhelming. A child might misinterpret a friend's teasing as hostility, leading to conflict or withdrawal. Role-playing scenarios at home can help prepare them for various social situations, equipping them with the tools they need to navigate complex interactions more smoothly.

Academic pressures and expectations are additional triggers worth noting. A seemingly simple math worksheet can become a source of immense frustration. The pressure to perform, combined with a potential difficulty in focusing, culminates in an emotional response. Here, breaking tasks into smaller, more manageable chunks can make a huge difference. Offering frequent breaks and positive reinforcement further eases the pressure and boosts their confidence.

It's also important to recognize the role of physical states in triggering emotional responses. Hunger, fatigue, or even minor illnesses can amplify irritability and reduce a child's ability to cope with stressors. Ensuring regular meals, a good night's sleep, and staying attuned to their physical health are foundational steps in managing their emotional well- being.

Another factor often overlooked is the atmosphere at home. Family conflicts or high-stress environments can exacerbate emotional instability. Taking proactive measures to maintain a peaceful, respectful, and understanding household sets the tone for better emotional management. If arguments or disagreements arise, resolving them calmly and constructively in front of your child provides a strong model for handling conflict.

Structured activities can sometimes turn into unexpected triggers, too. Take holiday gatherings, for instance. What's meant to be a joyous occasion can spiral into a hotbed of stress due to changes in routine, unfamiliar faces, and sensory overload. Preparing your child by discussing the schedule of events in advance and setting up quiet spaces for breaks can mitigate the chaos.

It's crucial to note that not all triggers are negative. Positive stimuli, if not managed properly, can also lead to overstimulation. Think of a birthday party overflowing with excitement and activities—the high energy can flip from exhilarating to overwhelming in an instant. Monitoring their threshold can help keep joyous occasions joyful, without the emotional fallout.

Discipline strategies themselves can be mysterious triggers. Traditional punitive measures, like time-outs, might inadvertently heighten anxiety and perpetuate emotional spirals. Instead, positive reinforcement and natural consequences align more closely with a supportive environment that acknowledges the unique needs of children with ADHD.

Observing your child's reactions and keeping a trigger diary can be immensely helpful. Documenting the circumstances surrounding emotional outbursts provides valuable insights into what might be setting them off. Over time, patterns will emerge, offering a roadmap for interventions that can preemptively address these triggers.

Collaboration with educators and caregivers is vital. They can offer additional perspectives and information regarding behaviors that occur outside the home. A unified, consistent approach across various environments ensures that strategies to recognize and manage triggers are cohesive and effective. Regular communication between all parties can also help in adjusting techniques to suit changing needs.

Alongside recognizing triggers, building resilience and coping mechanisms is equally important. Teaching mindfulness practices and relaxation techniques can empower your child to manage their emotional responses proactively. Simple breathing exercises, for example, can be a go-to tool in moments of stress.

In conclusion, recognizing triggers is a multifaceted process that requires careful observation, consistent documentation, and a collaborative approach. By identifying what sets off emotional responses, you can take proactive measures to create a supportive environment that fosters emotional stability and resilience in children with ADHD. This foundational understanding will serve as a cornerstone for effective coping strategies and mindfulness practices, enabling your child to navigate their world with greater ease and confidence.

Coping Strategies

When it comes to managing emotions, one of the most vital ingredients is having a toolbox of effective coping strategies. Coping strategies are like navigation tools; they help children with ADHD steer through the turbulent waters of emotional upheaval. Fortunately, helping kids with ADHD develop these skills can make a significant difference in their daily lives. Below, we'll discuss some practical and actionable methods that can be seamlessly integrated into daily routines.

First and foremost, it is essential to teach children emotional awareness. This involves helping them recognize their emotions and understand what triggers them. A simple yet effective way to do this is by using an emotional chart. You might ask your child to point to or name the emotion they're feeling. Over time, this practice can make them more attuned to their emotional landscape, which is the first step in managing it effectively.

Another fundamental strategy involves deep breathing exercises. Deep breathing can serve as a quick and efficient way to alleviate stress and anxiety. Children can be taught to take a deep breath through their nose, hold it for a few seconds, and then exhale slowly through their mouth. Practicing this simple exercise regularly can make it easier for them to implement in moments of emotional distress.

Physical activity can also work wonders as a coping mechanism. Activities such as running, jumping, or even dancing can help release pent-up energy and improve mood. Encouraging regular physical activity in your child's routine can serve as a preventive measure against emotional flare-ups.

Creating a "calm-down" space is another effective coping strategy. Think of it as an emotional safe haven where a child can retreat when they need to cool down. This space can be filled with comforting items like soft pillows, calming books, or even a favorite stuffed animal. Allowing children to take a break in this designated area can help them regain their composure more quickly.

Sometimes, distraction is the best form of coping. Having a go-to list of enjoyable activities can provide a quick way for a child to shift their focus away from the emotional trigger. This could be anything from listening to music, drawing, or even playing a quick game. The idea is to offer an immediate outlet that takes their mind off whatever was causing the emotional distress.

It's also beneficial to use stories and role-playing scenarios to teach emotional regulation. Reading stories that discuss different emotions or acting out various scenarios can give children practical examples of how to handle their feelings. This method not only engages their imagination but also provides context-specific strategies that they can use in real-life situations.

Sometimes, offering sensory-based interventions can be very helpful. Items like stress balls, fidget spinners, or textured fabrics can provide sensory input that calms the nervous system. These can serve as discreet, yet effective tools for self-regulation that children can use anytime, anywhere.

Open communication plays a crucial role in emotional management. Encourage your child to talk about their feelings by setting aside a few minutes each day for a "feelings check-in." This could be during a calm moment at the end of the day or even as part of the bedtime routine. When children are given the opportunity to express their emotions regularly, it reduces the likelihood of emotional outbursts.

You might also want to consider incorporating mindfulness practices into your child's daily schedule. Simple mindfulness exercises, such as focusing on their breath or paying attention to their surroundings, can help improve their emotional resilience. Mindfulness can train them to stay grounded in the present moment, making it easier to deal with emotional highs and lows.

Problem-solving skills are another important aspect of emotional coping. Teaching children a step-by-step approach to solve problems can help them feel more in control when emotions run high. You can break down a problem into smaller, manageable steps and guide your child in coming up with solutions. This structured approach can reduce feelings of overwhelm and build confidence.

Finally, it is important to celebrate small victories. Positive reinforcement can go a long way in encouraging children to use coping strategies effectively. Every time they successfully manage their emotions, acknowledge their effort and progress. This not only boosts their self- esteem but also reinforces the positive behavior.

In summary, fostering a variety of coping strategies can make a remarkable difference in how children with ADHD manage their emotions. From deep breathing and physical activity to creating calm-down spaces and practicing mindfulness, these strategies offer practical and actionable ways to help children navigate their emotional landscape more effectively. By providing these tools and encouraging their use, you can help your child develop into a more emotionally resilient individual.

Mindfulness Practices

Mindfulness isn't just a buzzword; it's a powerful tool that can help manage emotions and bring peace to both children and adults grappling with ADHD. The practice of mindfulness involves paying attention to the present moment without judgment. This might sound simple, but it can be incredibly effective for children with ADHD, who often struggle with staying present and regulating their emotions.

One of the key components of mindfulness practice is mindfulness meditation. Teaching children how to meditate can help them develop the ability to observe their thoughts and feelings without getting overwhelmed by them. Start small! A one-minute meditation session can work wonders. Over time, as the child becomes more comfortable, you can gradually increase the duration. Remember, the goal is not perfection but progress. Stressing over getting it "right" can counteract the benefits.

Consider incorporating breathing exercises. Simple practices like deep breathing can significantly reduce anxiety and improve focus. You might try the "5-5-5" technique: inhale for five seconds, hold for five seconds, and then exhale for five seconds. This practice can be done anywhere and anytime, making it a versatile tool in emotional management. You can also make it fun by turning it into a game or a routine part of their day.

Mindfulness doesn't have to be a solo activity. Group mindfulness exercises can be beneficial as well. Practicing mindfulness as a family can create a shared sense of calm and connection. For example, take a mindful walk together. This involves walking slowly and paying attention to the sensation of your feet touching the ground, the sounds around you, and the feeling of the breeze on your skin. Discuss what each family member noticed during the walk; this can enhance your bond while cultivating mindfulness.

Storytelling can also serve as an effective mindfulness practice. Reading stories that incorporate mindful characters or passages can teach children how to apply mindfulness in everyday situations. Moreover, it encourages empathy by helping them understand other perspectives and feelings.

Another engaging way to include mindfulness is through creative activities. Drawing, painting, or even building with blocks can be turned into mindful exercises. Encourage children to focus on each brushstroke, each pencil mark, or the way the blocks fit together. As they concentrate on their activity, they learn to enjoy the process rather than rushing to the completion.

Use technology to your advantage. There are numerous apps available designed to teach mindfulness and meditation specifically for children. These apps often include guided meditations, short mindfulness exercises, and even games that encourage mindful thinking. Just be sure to monitor screen time and balance these activities with non-digital mindfulness practices.

Incorporate mindfulness during transitional periods to help ease anxiety, which is particularly beneficial for children with ADHD who often struggle with changes in routine. Whether it's moving from one classroom to another, getting ready for bed, or preparing to leave the house, a few minutes of mindfulness can make these transitions smoother. Simple practices like focusing on the breath or a quick body scan can make a difference.

Mindfulness practices can also be integrated into school routines. Teachers can lead short mindfulness exercises at the beginning or end of the day or before tests to help students manage stress and improve focus. Encouraging students to take mindfulness breaks can foster a more calm and productive learning environment, benefiting all students, especially those with ADHD.

Gratitude exercises can be a form of mindfulness practice. Encourage children to list three things they are grateful for each day. This shifts their focus from negative thoughts to positive ones, helping them build a more optimistic perspective. It's a simple yet effective way to foster emotional well-being and can easily become a daily family ritual.

Being mindful also means being aware of and addressing emotional triggers. Encourage children to name their emotions ("I feel sad," "I am angry") and observe them without judgment. This can help them distance themselves from the intensity of these feelings and manage them better. Over time, they'll become more adept at recognizing emotions as they arise, leading to more proactive emotional management.

Another powerful tool is the use of mindful affirmations. Creating a set of positive affirmations that children can repeat to themselves can bolster their self-esteem and help regulate their emotions. Phrases like "I am calm," "I can handle this," and "I am in control of my emotions," can be incredibly powerful when repeated regularly. These affirmations help in rewiring the brain toward more positive thinking.

It's essential for parents and caregivers to model mindfulness themselves. Children are more likely to adopt these practices if they see adults doing them too. Whether it's taking a deep breath before reacting to a stressful situation or practising gratitude, your actions will speak louder than words. By demonstrating mindfulness, you're encouraging your child to follow suit.

In conclusion, integrating mindfulness practices into daily routines can provide numerous benefits for managing emotions, particularly for children with ADHD. These practices are practical, easy to implement, and can be varied to keep them engaging. Remember, the aim is to cultivate a more peaceful and aware state of mind, making it easier to navigate the often turbulent waters of emotional management.

Chapter 10:
Navigating Medication

When it comes to ADHD, medication is often a topic that brings both relief and angst. It's a path many families consider but deciding to start medication isn't always straightforward. This chapter aims to shine a light on the intricacies, providing you with a clearer understanding to navigate this complex terrain.

Understanding medication options is crucial. First, it's worth noting that there are two primary categories: stimulants and non-stimulants. Stimulants, such as methylphenidate and amphetamine-based medications, are the most commonly prescribed. They work by increasing the levels of certain neurotransmitters in the brain which aid in improving concentration and reducing impulsivity. Non-stimulants, on the other hand, like atomoxetine and certain antidepressants, don't act as quickly but can be effective for some children.

Parents often have valid concerns about side effects. Stimulants can sometimes lead to decreased appetite, sleep difficulties, or increased anxiety. Non-stimulants might cause fatigue or stomach issues. It's essential to remember that no two children react the same way, so what works for one child might not work for another. This variability underscores the importance of working closely with healthcare providers to monitor and adjust medication as needed.

Weighing the pros and cons of medication involves considering both the potential benefits and the possible drawbacks. One of the significant advantages is that medication can provide much-needed relief from symptoms, which can lead to improved academic performance, better social interactions, and increased self-esteem. The downside is managing side effects and the trial-and-error process of finding the right dosage and medication type.

It's wise to think of medication as one tool in a broader ADHD management toolkit. Medication can be highly effective, especially when combined with behavioral therapy, structured routines, and supportive interventions at school and home. This combination often yields the best results, helping children thrive in multiple areas.

Communication with healthcare providers is paramount. Establishing a strong partnership with your child's doctor can make a notable difference. Regular check-ins and open dialogues about what is and isn't working are vital. Don't be afraid to voice concerns, ask questions, or request adjustments in treatment. Remember, you are your child's biggest advocate.

It's also helpful to understand that starting medication isn't a one-time decision but rather an ongoing process. From initial considerations and consultations to trying out different medications and dosages, it takes time. Patience is key, as finding the right balance might mean facing a few bumps along the way.

Parents often grapple with feelings of guilt or anxiety about medicating their child. It's perfectly normal to worry about making the "right" decision. Many find it beneficial to join support groups where sharing experiences and gaining insights from others in similar situations can be comforting and enlightening. There's a unique strength in community and shared experiences can often shed light on your own journey.

It's also worth addressing some myths surrounding ADHD medication. One common misconception is that medication will alter a child's personality or "zombify" them. While adjustments in behavior can occur, the goal is always to help the child become the best version of themselves, not to suppress their individuality. Properly managed medication should aid in reducing the challenges ADHD presents while allowing the child's personality to shine through.

Lastly, setting realistic expectations about what medication can achieve is important. It's not a cure but a means to manage symptoms more effectively. Success with medication looks different for each child - for some, it might mean fewer meltdowns, for others, it might mean better focus in school.

So as you navigate this critical aspect of ADHD management, recall that an open mind, a heart full of patience, and a supportive network can make this journey far more manageable. With the right information and support, finding the right medication can transform challenges into opportunities for meaningful development.

Understanding medication options, weighing the pros and cons, partnering with healthcare providers, and staying informed can all contribute to a positive outcome. It's a nuanced path, but with diligence and care, you can help your child thrive, medication being one of the key tools that you thoughtfully and compassionately utilize.

Understanding Options

When it comes to ADHD medication, choosing the right option can feel like navigating a maze. You've got an array of choices, each with its own set of benefits and challenges. Understanding these options is crucial to making an informed decision that's tailored to the unique needs of your child. So, let's break it down.

First, there's the distinction between stimulant and non-stimulant medications. Stimulants, like Adderall and Ritalin, are often considered the first line of treatment for ADHD. They work by increasing the levels of certain chemicals in the brain that help control attention and behavior. On the flip side, non-stimulants like Strattera and Intuniv offer an alternative, especially for kids who don't respond well to stimulants or experience too many side effects. Understanding these categories provides a foundation upon which you can build your knowledge about ADHD medication.

Medications also come in various forms and delivery methods, which can impact their effectiveness and how easily they fit into your child's routine. Some are long-acting, providing symptom control throughout the day, while others are short-acting and may require multiple doses. For example, some kids might do well with a long-acting capsule taken in the morning, while others may benefit from a short-acting tablet that can be taken multiple times a day. There are even liquid and chewable forms for those who have difficulty swallowing pills. The key is to find the right form that fits seamlessly into your family's daily life.

Another option worth considering is the timing of medication. Some families find that administering medication during school days helps to manage academic and social challenges, but they opt for medication holidays on weekends or summer breaks. This approach allows for a balance between managing symptoms and minimizing potential side effects. However, it's essential to consult with your healthcare provider to determine if this strategy is suitable for your child.

Side effects are an inevitable part of the conversation when discussing medication. Stimulant medications can sometimes cause appetite loss, sleep issues, or even increased anxiety. Non-stimulants have their own set of potential side effects like fatigue or mood swings. It's crucial to weigh these considerations and understand that finding the optimal medication often involves some trial and error. Regular follow-ups with your healthcare provider are essential to monitoring and tweaking the treatment plan as needed.

Another aspect to navigate is the concept of combination therapy, where medication is used alongside other treatments such as behavioral therapy. Medication can help manage symptoms, making it easier for your child to benefit from behavioral interventions, educational support, and other non- pharmacological treatments. This holistic approach can often yield the best results, creating a more comprehensive management plan for ADHD.

In addition to traditional medications, there are alternative options that some families explore. These include dietary supplements, herbal remedies, and lifestyle changes like improved diet and exercise. While these alternatives may not replace medication, they can sometimes play a complementary role. Always consult with a healthcare provider before introducing any new treatments to ensure they are safe and effective for your child.

It's also important to be aware of the legal and ethical considerations surrounding medication. This includes understanding the regulations about prescription medications, especially for controlled substances like stimulants. Keeping open lines of communication with your child's school and caregivers can also help ensure that the medication plan is implemented smoothly and responsibly.

Finally, talk openly with your child about their medication. Empowering them with knowledge helps to demystify the process and can make them more receptive to treatment. Encourage them to share how they're feeling and discuss any side effects they may be experiencing. This ongoing dialogue can significantly contribute to finding the most effective medication plan.

Navigating medication options for ADHD can be challenging, but it's a journey worth taking. With the right resources, support, and a bit of patience, you'll find an approach that works best for your child. Remember, you're not alone in this – healthcare providers, educators, and support groups are all there to help guide you through this complex landscape.

Weighing Pros and Cons

When it comes to managing ADHD, medication often comes up as a significant point of discussion. It's like being at a crossroads, and you've got to pick a path that may influence your child's future. While medication isn't a magic bullet, it can be a key component in a broader strategy for managing ADHD. This section aims to provide a nuanced look at the potential benefits and drawbacks of medication, so you're better informed when making this vital decision.

First off, let's talk about the potential upsides. ADHD medications, particularly stimulants like methylphenidate and amphetamines, can produce noticeable improvements in focus, attention, and impulse control relatively quickly. For children struggling academically or socially, these changes can be nothing short of transformative. Improved focus can lead to better performance in school and more meaningful interactions with both peers and family members. Essentially, the right medication can act as a sort of bridge, helping children overcome some of the neurological challenges that come with ADHD.

But before we get too carried away with the upside, it's crucial to remember that not all children respond to medication in the same way. What's effective for one child might not be for another. This variability can make the process feel a bit like trial and error, which can be frustrating for both parents and children. Additionally, medications like stimulants can have side effects. Common ones include loss of appetite, difficulty sleeping, and mood swings. These side effects may dissipate over time but not always. For some families, the side effects can outweigh the benefits, leading to the difficult decision of stopping medication altogether.

Now, let's switch gears and talk about non-stimulant medications, such as atomoxetine or guanfacine. These can be a viable alternative for children who either don't respond well to stimulants or experience severe side effects. Non-stimulants typically have a different side effect profile and may not produce benefits as rapidly. However, they can still be effective in managing ADHD symptoms, especially when accompanied by behavioral therapies and other non-pharmacological interventions. The slower onset of action can be a double-edged sword; while it might mean fewer side effects, it also means families need to exercise more patience to see if the medication will be effective.

Another significant factor to weigh is the long-term impact of medication on a child's development. While immediate benefits like improved focus and behavior can be apparent, there's some debate about the long-term effects of ADHD medications. Some research indicates that consistent medication use can lead to long-term improvements in academic and social functioning. However, other studies suggest potential drawbacks, such as the impact on growth rates or cardiovascular health, although more research is needed to draw definitive conclusions. This uncertainty can add another layer of complexity to the decision-making process.

Then there's the social and emotional aspect of medication. Kids are perceptive, and they often understand more than we give them credit for. The decision to medicate can sometimes affect a child's self-perception. Some might feel stigmatized or different from their peers, which can impact their self-esteem. It's essential to have open and honest conversations with your child about why they're taking medication and how it can help them. Empowering them with this knowledge can mitigate some of the emotional downsides.

Lastly, consider the logistics and financial aspects. ADHD medications can be expensive, particularly if you're still in the trial and error phase and trying different options. Insurance might cover some of the costs, but not always. Further, regular doctor visits for prescription refills and monitoring add another layer of commitment. It's not just about popping a pill; it's an ongoing process that involves adjustments, follow-ups, and sometimes advocating for your child in the healthcare system.

In sum, the decision to use medication for ADHD management is anything but straightforward. It involves a complex weighing of pros and cons, ranging from immediate behavioral improvements to potential long-term impacts. On the upside, medication can provide fast, noticeable relief from some of ADHD's most disruptive symptoms, significantly enhancing a child's quality of life. On the downside, side effects, variability in response, and long-term uncertainties make it a less-than- perfect solution. Ultimately, the goal isn't necessarily to find a "fix," but to equip your child with the best tools possible to navigate their world more effectively. Collaborating closely with healthcare providers, educators, and most importantly, your child, can make this journey a bit smoother.

Working with Healthcare Providers

Once you've decided to explore medication as an option for managing ADHD, working with healthcare providers becomes an essential part of the journey. Navigating this relationship can feel overwhelming, but knowing what to expect and how to communicate effectively can make a significant difference.

First off, it's crucial to understand the role of healthcare providers in the ADHD medication process. Typically, this team includes pediatricians, psychiatrists, and sometimes neurologists. Each specialist has a different focus but works together to create a comprehensive treatment plan tailored to your child's needs. Pediatricians often handle initial assessments and general health, while psychiatrists specialize in psychiatric disorders and can provide detailed medication management.

It's important to recognize that you are an active participant in this team. You know your child best and can provide valuable insights into their behavior, triggers, and what strategies have or have not worked in the past. This collaborative approach can help healthcare providers make more informed decisions regarding your child's treatment.

When preparing for your first appointment, gather any previous medical records, school reports, or behavioral assessments. Having a detailed account of your child's symptoms, daily routines, and any past interventions can be incredibly useful. This not only helps the provider understand the situation better but also sets a solid foundation for tracking progress over time.

Communication is key during these consultations. Don't be afraid to ask questions or seek clarification on anything you don't understand. Medication, especially for ADHD, can come with a lot of jargon—terms like "stimulants," "non-stimulants," "side effects," and "dosages" can be daunting. A good healthcare provider won't mind taking the time to explain these concepts in plain language.

Now, what about those tough conversations regarding potential side effects? It's natural to be concerned about how medication might impact your child's physical and emotional well-being. Open a candid dialogue with your healthcare provider about these concerns. Discuss common side effects, monitor how your child responds to the medication, and never hesitate to report any adverse reactions. Every child is unique, and what works for one may not work for another. Keeping an open line of communication can lead to adjustments in dosage or even a change in medication if necessary.

If you're continuously hitting roadblocks or aren't seeing the desired results, it might be time to seek a second opinion. This doesn't mean you don't trust your current provider; rather, it's about being thorough and getting the best care for your child. A different perspective or expertise may offer new solutions you hadn't considered.

Navigating insurance can be a maze all its own. Many healthcare plans require specific referrals or only cover certain specialists. Make sure you're well-versed in your insurance policy to avoid unexpected costs. Always ask about costs upfront, and if your current provider isn't covered by your insurance, don't hesitate to search for alternatives that align with your financial situation.

Now, let's talk about follow-up visits. Consistency is crucial when managing ADHD with medication. Regular check-ups allow healthcare providers to monitor how well the medication is working and make necessary adjustments. These visits are also an excellent opportunity to discuss any new behaviors, ongoing concerns, or additional support your child might need.

Your child's input in these healthcare interactions is equally essential. Encourage them to express how they feel on the medication honestly. Sometimes, side effects or challenges become apparent through their feedback. This direct communication helps personalize the treatment plan further and ensures your child feels heard and involved.

In addition to medication management, healthcare providers can offer a wealth of resources and referrals. They can guide you toward support groups, educational workshops, or behavioral therapy options. Many parents find that a combination of medication and behavioral strategies works best for their child, and healthcare providers can be instrumental in coordinating this multifaceted approach.

Let's not forget the role of school personnel in this entire process. Often, teachers and school nurses interact with your child throughout the day and can provide valuable insights into how the medication affects them in various settings. Share any relevant medical information with the school staff and ensure there's a streamlined communication channel between them and your healthcare provider.

Some healthcare providers may suggest genetic testing to better understand how your child metabolizes medication. While this isn't a standard practice, in certain cases, it can offer additional insights into the most effective treatment options. Discuss the pros and cons of such testing with your provider to make an informed decision.

Lastly, don't underestimate the power of community. Other parents going through similar experiences can provide moral support, share their journeys, and even offer practical advice. Healthcare providers often know of local or online support groups you can join, creating a network of understanding and shared experiences.

Working with healthcare providers isn't a one-time event; it's an ongoing partnership aimed at helping your child thrive. By staying informed, proactive, and communicative, you can navigate the complexities of medication with greater ease and confidence. This team effort can unlock your child's full potential, paving the way for a more balanced and fulfilling life.

Chapter 11:
Incorporating Physical Activity

Physical activity is not just a fun pastime for children; it's a game-changer, especially for those with ADHD. Engaging in regular exercise has shown to offer myriad benefits, from improving concentration and reducing impulsivity to boosting mood and overall well-being. Research suggests that physical activity can significantly help manage ADHD symptoms, making it an essential tool in your parenting toolbox.

Now, you might be wondering, what kind of activities are the best fit for kids with ADHD? The answer isn't one-size-fits-all. What's important is that the activities should be enjoyable and engaging for your child. If they love what they're doing, they're more likely to stick with it. Whether it's a team sport like soccer or an individual activity like swimming, finding that sweet spot can make all the difference.

One of the beauties of physical exercise is its variety. For some kids, structured sports work wonders. The rules and routines of a sport can provide just enough structure to keep them focused. For others, less structured activities might be more appealing. A simple game of tag, bike rides around the neighborhood, or even jumping on a trampoline can provide the physical outlet they need.

But, it's not just about the type of activity; it's also about balancing their activity levels. Too little exercise can leave them restless and fidgety, while overdoing it can lead to burnout. Striking a balance is key.

Incorporate short bursts of activity throughout the day if long sessions seem daunting. A quick 10-minute dance party, a brief walk after meals, or even a five-minute stretch can break up the monotony and re-energize your child. These mini-workouts can be just as effective as a longer session.

Remember, leading by example is powerful. If you're active, your child is more likely to be active too. So, lace up those sneakers, and make physical activity a family affair! The benefits you'll all gain go beyond just managing ADHD symptoms. Regular exercise promotes a healthier lifestyle, improves mental clarity, and builds lasting family bonds.

Ultimately, the goal is to weave physical activity seamlessly into your daily routine. Not only will it help manage ADHD symptoms, but it'll also provide a healthy outlet for energy and emotions. So let's get moving!

Benefits of Exercise

Getting kids with ADHD to exercise regularly isn't just about burning off excess energy—though that's certainly a benefit. Exercise has a slew of advantages that go beyond just the physical. The beauty of incorporating physical activity lies in its multifaceted benefits that enhance not only body but also mind and spirit. In this section, we'll explore why making exercise a part of your child's daily routine can be a game-changer.

First off, let's talk about the immediate physical perks. Regular exercise helps improve cardiovascular health, muscle strength, and flexibility. Children with ADHD often have a lot of energy, and regular physical activity gives them a positive outlet for it. When those bursts of energy are channeled into productive, physical exertion, it also inherently decreases the likelihood of disruptive behavior.

Moreover, the benefits aren't merely skin-deep. Exercise triggers the release of endorphins, the body's natural mood lifters. This can significantly reduce feelings of anxiety and depression, common co-occurring conditions in children with ADHD. The simple act of moving around and getting the heart rate up allows for the release of these happiness-boosting chemicals, leading to a natural sense of euphoria and well-being.

Another point worth noting is how exercise impacts cognitive function. Studies have shown that physical activity enhances brain function and neuroplasticity, which means your child's brain becomes better at adapting and learning. Exercise improves blood flow to the brain and encourages the growth of new brain cells, particularly in the hippocampus, the area associated with memory and learning. Enhanced brain function leads to improved focus, better problem-solving skills, and heightened creativity. It's not magic, but it's close!

Exercise also has a positive effect on executive function, which includes skills like planning, organization, and time management—all areas often challenging for kids with ADHD. By incorporating regular physical activity into daily routines, these skills can naturally and gradually improve. Thus, physical activity becomes a vital component in a holistic approach to managing ADHD symptoms.

Consistent exercise helps regulate sleep patterns, another crucial factor in managing ADHD. Many children with ADHD struggle with sleep disorders, which can exacerbate symptoms and make daytime functioning even more challenging. Regular physical activity helps to tire the body out naturally, making it easier for children to fall asleep and stay asleep. Better rest means better mood and attention span the next day, creating a positive cycle.

Let's not forget the social aspect of exercise. Team sports and group activities provide opportunities for children to develop essential social skills. Children learn how to communicate, cooperate, and resolve conflicts while engaging in a physically active setting. This social interaction can be invaluable, providing a structured environment where kids can practice and enhance their social abilities.

Additionally, participating in sports and physical activities gives children a sense of accomplishment and boosts their self-esteem. Scoring a goal in soccer, finishing a dance routine, or simply running a faster mile gives tangible proof of effort and success. These achievements, no matter how small, accumulate to foster a positive self-image and a sense of pride.

Physical routines also serve as excellent anchors of structure and discipline. For kids with ADHD, more predictability in their day can decrease anxiety and improve overall behavior. Scheduled exercise times, whether it's morning jogs, afternoon sports, or evening yoga, provide a steady rhythm to the day that can be extremely comforting. Knowing what to expect next helps children transition between activities more smoothly.

Last but not least, let's talk about fun and enjoyment. Exercise doesn't have to be a chore. Finding an activity that your child genuinely enjoys can turn "exercise time" into a highlight of the day. When children look forward to physical activity, it becomes easier to incorporate it consistently into their routines. The joy of movement and play should not be underestimated; it is intrinsic to childhood and can have lasting positive effects on mental and physical health.

Incorporating physical activity is much more than just a strategy to manage excess energy in kids with ADHD. It's a holistic solution that offers benefits ranging from improved physical health to enhanced cognitive function and social skills. It's about crafting a balanced, enriching lifestyle that supports, nurtures, and empowers your child to thrive. Keep exploring various activities to find what resonates best with your child, and make physical activity a joyful and enduring part of their daily life.

Finding Enjoyable Activities

You've likely heard it a hundred times: "Get your kids active!" Sure, sounds simple enough, but the larger challenge often lies in finding enjoyable activities that capture your child's attention and keep them coming back for more. Especially for children with ADHD, the activity needs to be engaging enough to hold their interest. And let's face it, getting them to stick with something that's as fun as watching paint dry just isn't going to cut it.

First things first—let's toss out the notion that physical activity has to be structured. While traditional sports like soccer and basketball are great, they aren't necessarily a one-size-fits-all solution. Would it surprise you if I told you that something as unconventional as rock climbing or even dancing can do wonders? The key is to flip the script and think beyond the usual suspects.

Take a step back and observe what naturally draws your child's attention. Are they scrambling up trees whenever they get the chance? That's a hint they might love rock climbing. Do they bounce around to music? Maybe a dance class is more their speed. By zeroing in on these natural inclinations, you're more likely to find an activity that they enjoy and, more importantly, stick with.

Speaking of sticking with it, let's talk about how to make these activities a lasting part of their routine. Consistency is essential, but variety can be equally important. Sure, your child might love swimming now, but in a few months, they could be tired of doing laps. The trick is to keep a mix of activities on hand so there's always something new and exciting on the horizon.

Understanding your child's social preferences can also help tailor activities to their needs. Some children thrive in team sports where they can work collaboratively with others. This could be soccer, baseball, or even quirky team-building exercises like relay races. On the flip side, if your child needs personal space to shine, solitary activities like swimming, cycling, or tennis might be a better fit.

Introducing them to a variety of activities not only keeps things fresh but also helps them develop a range of skills—both physically and socially. Participating in team sports, for instance, teaches teamwork and communication, while solitary activities, like martial arts, can improve focus and self-discipline.

Incorporating physical activity into daily family routines can also give you a break while promoting healthy habits. Family hikes, weekend bike rides, or even an evening of dancing in the living room can make physical activity a fun, interactive part of daily life. Plus, when you participate, you're modeling healthy behavior, making it more likely that your child will continue these activities independently.

Let's not overlook the power of choice, either. Giving your child a say in picking the activity can significantly increase their buy-in. Instead of dictating which sports or exercises they need to do, present them with a menu of options. "Do you want to try rollerblading or would you prefer going for a run?" This simple act of choosing empowers them and makes them more invested in the outcome.

Balancing screen time and physical activity is another crucial aspect you'll need to navigate. It's easy for kids to get sucked into the vortex of video games and TV, but creating a reward system where screen time is earned through physical activity can offer a balanced approach. For example, thirty minutes of basketball could earn them an equal amount of screen time.

If your child has a natural bent toward technology, leveraging apps and games that encourage movement can be a win-win. Augmented Reality (AR) games, where they have to walk around to progress in the game, can be incredibly motivating. For instance, games like Pokémon

GO prompt your child to explore the neighborhood, combining physical activity with digital incentives.

Not every child is going to have an instant connection with physical activities. Sometimes, a gentle nudge is necessary. Encourage sampling different activities by maintaining an open dialogue about what they liked or disliked about each one. This feedback can guide you in fine-tuning your approach and finding that "aha" activity that clicks.

Lastly, incentive programs can play an essential role. Maybe it's earning stickers for every week of consistent activity, which build up to a larger reward like a new toy or a special outing. These small incentives can boost motivation and help make physical activity a regular part of their routine.

And here's the thing—this journey doesn't have to be perfect. There will be days when your child just isn't in the mood, and that's okay. The goal is not to create Olympic athletes but to instill a lifelong love for movement, paving the way for healthier habits that will serve them well into adulthood.

Finding enjoyable activities is less about sticking to a rigid plan and more about flexibility, understanding, and a touch of creativity. By paying attention to what naturally excites your child, giving them choices, and keeping the experience varied and fun, you'll be setting the stage for a more active and fulfilling life.

Balancing Activity Levels

When it comes to balancing activity levels for children with ADHD, it's a blend of art and science. Too much activity can lead to burnout and frustration, too little and you risk the pitfalls of sedentary behavior—think lack of focus and a rise in hyperactivity. It's all about getting that sweet spot where kids are engaged, energized, and able to channel their energy in productive ways. But how does one navigate this delicate balance? Let's dive into some practical strategies that can seamlessly fit into daily routines.

First, let's acknowledge that every child is different. What works for one may not work for another, and that's okay. Some kids might thrive with a high-energy routine packed with sports, dance, and more, while others might need their activities spread throughout the day. Observing your child's natural rhythms can give you valuable insights into what they need. Pay attention to when they seem most restless or most focused, and tailor their activity schedule accordingly.

A good starting point is to integrate short bursts of physical activity into the day. Rather than one long session, consider breaking up the exercise into manageable chunks. For example, a quick game of tag before school, a bike ride after lunch, and a bit of trampoline time before dinner. These mini-sessions can help keep kids engaged without overwhelming them. Plus, it often provides the added benefit of breaking up long periods of sedentary time, which can be particularly challenging for children with ADHD.

It's also essential to ensure the activities are enjoyable for the child. Let them have a say in what they want to do. Whether it's soccer, swimming, or even a family hike, the key is to make sure they're having fun. This not only keeps them motivated but also helps build a positive association with physical activity, making it something they look forward to rather than a chore.

And don't underestimate the power of variety. Mixing up activities can prevent boredom and keep children engaged. One day it could be basketball, the next day yoga or a nature walk. The goal is to keep the physical activity diverse and stimulating, so the child doesn't lose interest.

However, it's not just about the quantity of physical activity, but also the quality. Structured activities like martial arts or team sports can be great for providing a regimented form of exercise that carries the added benefits of discipline and social interaction. Conversely, unstructured play like free time at the park or backyard antics also has its place— stimulating creativity and providing a healthy outlet for energy.

While you're balancing activity levels, it's crucial to watch for signs of both under- and over-exertion. Indicators like mood swings, fatigue, or a child showing disinterest in activities they normally enjoy can be red flags. Constantly re-evaluating and adjusting the schedule based on your child's feedback and behavior is key. There's no one-size-fits-all approach, so flexibility is your best friend here.

Parents might also consider mind-body activities that combine physical movement with mental focus. Exercises like yoga or tai chi can be fantastic for children with ADHD. These practices not only help in physical conditioning but also in developing concentration and calmness, which are invaluable skills for managing ADHD symptoms.

Balancing activity levels isn't just about the kids, though—parents play a crucial role, too. Modeling an active lifestyle can have a significant impact. If children see their parents engaging in physical activities and enjoying them, it sends a powerful message. Plus, family activities can double as quality bonding time, killing two birds with one stone. Imagine a weekend family hike or a daily post-dinner stroll together. These moments can become cherished rituals that promote both physical health and family unity.

Lastly, let's talk about integrating physical activity without it feeling forced. Simple adaptations can make a big difference. Opt for walking or biking to school instead of driving, or turn household chores into fun activities. Even something as simple as dancing to a favorite song while cleaning up can make the task more enjoyable and inject some physical activity into the day.

In summary, balancing activity levels for children with ADHD revolves around variety, enjoyment, and flexibility. Observe your child's natural rhythms, break activities into manageable chunks, and make sure they have a say in what they do. Mix up structured and unstructured play, incorporate mind-body practices, and lead by example. These strategies not only help in managing ADHD symptoms but also cultivate a love for physical activity that can benefit your child's overall well-being.

Chapter 12:
Family Therapy Insights

When navigating the complex world of ADHD, it's easy to forget that the entire family dynamic is affected. You're not just dealing with one individual's symptoms; you're managing the ripple effect that ADHD creates within family relationships. Understanding the role of family dynamics in ADHD is crucial. Often, the most successful interventions are those that involve the whole family rather than placing the burden solely on one person.

Family therapy offers some much-needed insight into how ADHD can strain familial relationships and, importantly, how to mend and strengthen these bonds. One key aspect that can't be overlooked is the necessity for everyone to be on the same page. Family members must adopt a united front, which helps in mitigating feelings of isolation and misunderstanding that someone with ADHD might experience. Therapists act like coaches, helping families build a playbook tailored to their specific needs.

Choosing the right therapist can feel like finding a needle in a haystack, but it doesn't have to be daunting. First, look for a therapist who specializes in ADHD and family therapy. This expertise is invaluable because such a professional can provide nuanced advice that general practitioners might not. Checking credentials, seeking recommendations, and having a preliminary meeting can give you a good sense of whether the therapist will be a good fit for your family. After all, therapy is a partnership, and trust is essential.

Successful therapy techniques often emphasize the idea that small, incremental changes can yield the best results. Take the "sandwich technique," for example. This involves sandwiching a critical feedback with positive comments. It sounds simple but can make a world of difference in how your child perceives and accepts guidance. Equally important is the use of non-verbal cues—positive body language and facial expressions often speak louder than words.

Another technique used in family therapy is role reversal. This method allows family members to see things from each other's perspectives. Not only does it foster empathy, but it also helps everyone involved understand that behavior often stems from unmet needs or frustration rather than malice. This shift in perspective can foster a more compassionate and effective communication style within the family.

It's not just about the techniques, though. It's the commitment to regular sessions and the homework outside of those sessions that makes the real difference. Family therapy isn't a magic bullet, but think of it as a toolbox full of practical strategies that you can employ day-to-day. Consistency and effort are key.

Don't underestimate the importance of celebrating small victories. Whether it's your child successfully following a routine or siblings working through a disagreement without conflict, these moments are milestones. Therapy isn't just about addressing issues; it's also about recognizing and celebrating progress, no matter how small it may seem.

In sum, family therapy provides invaluable insights not only into managing ADHD but also into fostering a healthier and more supportive family environment. The therapist offers a mirror that reflects not just the challenges but also the strengths that each family member brings to the table. By embracing these insights and techniques, you can create a more harmonious home where everyone feels understood, valued, and supported.

The Role of Family Dynamics

When discussing the effectiveness of family therapy in addressing ADHD, one can't ignore the pivotal role that family dynamics play. Imagine a home as a bustling little ecosystem, where every member, from young to old, impacts and influences each other. This interconnectedness turns out to be both a challenge and an opportunity when managing ADHD in children.

First, let's consider the nature of ADHD itself. It's a condition marked by impulsivity, hyperactivity, and inattention. These symptoms don't exist in a vacuum; they ripple through every aspect of family life. Each day can present situations that test the patience, understanding, and flexibility of every member. This continuous, sometimes chaotic, ebb and flow often create strain but also sets the stage for remarkable growth.

One of the most significant aspects of family dynamics is the emotional climate in the home. Is the atmosphere calm or stressful? Open or closed? Warm or indifferent? ADHD can both influence and be influenced by these emotional undercurrents. Imagine trying to maintain focus in a stormy sea; that's what a child with ADHD might feel if their home environment is tense and unpredictable.

Consider also the parental roles. Parents naturally take on various roles: disciplinarian, nurturer, teacher, friend. But ADHD forces these roles to be more nuanced and balanced. A parent who is too authoritarian may stifle the child's self-expression, while one who is too permissive may fail to provide the structure the child needs. This balancing act requires constant vigilance, flexibility, and communication.

Communication, speaking of which, serves as the backbone of healthy family dynamics. In a family dealing with ADHD, clear, consistent communication is crucial. Simple things like regular family meetings, where everyone gets a chance to express their feelings and concerns, can work wonders. These meetings can help ensure that all family members feel heard and understood, making collective problem-solving more effective.

On top of that, siblings play an often understated but vital role. They can choose to be allies or critics, and their interactions can either alleviate or exacerbate the challenges associated with ADHD. Tasks like setting joint goals, engaging in cooperative play, and fostering a culture of mutual respect can all contribute positively. Siblings who understand the complexities of ADHD can become excellent supporters and advocates, not just within the family but in broader social contexts as well.

It's important to remember that family dynamics aren't just about handling problems; they are also about cultivating strengths. While ADHD brings challenges, it also brings unique talents and positive traits. Families who focus on celebrating strengths rather than just managing weaknesses tend to create a more supportive and uplifting atmosphere. Recognizing and nurturing these strengths can empower children and help them navigate their ADHD more effectively.

Another crucial point is the role of extended family. Grandparents, aunts, uncles—they all bring additional perspectives and support systems. Integrating these family members into the child's life can offer additional layers of emotional and even practical support. But it's essential to ensure that everyone is on the same page regarding the approaches and strategies employed to manage ADHD. Mixed messages from various adult figures can be confusing at best and counterproductive at worst.

Families must also reckon with societal influences. Peer pressure, educational systems, and social expectations all feed into family dynamics. Addressing these external factors often requires advocacy. Parents may find themselves in meetings with teachers, doctors, or other professionals to create a supportive broader environment for their child. Through advocacy, families not only improve their own situation but can also foster greater understanding and acceptance of ADHD in their communities.

Understanding the role of family dynamics in ADHD management opens avenues for targeted, effective therapeutic interventions. Therapists can tailor their strategies to the unique emotional and relational fabric of each family. Sessions might focus on improving communication, establishing consistent routines, or finding new ways to celebrate and utilize the ADHD child's unique strengths.

Through therapy, families can also develop coping mechanisms suited to their specific dynamics. For instance, mindfulness practices can help reduce overall stress levels, while role-playing scenarios can prepare the family for real-life challenges. These sessions provide a safe space for testing out new strategies and receiving constructive feedback. Over time, therapy helps to install a more harmonious and effective family dynamic, benefiting everyone involved.

We shouldn't overlook the role of self-care in these dynamics. Parents particularly need to remember that taking care of their own mental and physical health is crucial. A parent's well-being directly affects their ability to support and care for a child with ADHD. It's the classic "put your oxygen mask on first" principle but applied to family life.

In conclusion, family dynamics play a central role in managing ADHD. They shape the emotional climate, influence the effectiveness of communication, and determine the overall atmosphere of the home. By understanding and actively improving these dynamics, families can create a supportive, nurturing environment that enables children with ADHD to thrive. Family therapy becomes not just a tool but a transformative experience that binds the family unit closer together.

Choosing a Therapist

Choosing the right therapist for your family can feel like a daunting task, but it's one of the most crucial steps toward effectively managing ADHD within the family dynamic. The good news is that there are many professionals out there who specialize in ADHD and understand the unique challenges families face. Here's how to find the right fit.

First and foremost, it's essential to understand that not all therapists are created equal. Some specialize in cognitive-behavioral therapy (CBT), others in family systems therapy, and still others might focus on play therapy or mindfulness approaches. It's essential to identify what type of therapy is likely to benefit your family the most. Start by consulting with healthcare providers and asking for recommenddations. Word-of-mouth from trusted friends and family can also be invaluable.

Once you have a list of potential therapists, it's time to delve deeper. Check their credentials and make sure they have experience working with ADHD. Don't be afraid to ask pointed questions about their experience and approaches. The right therapist should be willing to discuss their methods and how they tailor those techniques to fit the unique needs of each family member.

One critical factor in choosing a therapist is their approach to family dynamics. ADHD affects more than the individual; it has ripple effects on parents, siblings, and even extended family members. The therapist should have a holistic view and a plan that involves the entire family. This often includes creating strategies for parents to use at home to build a supportive environment.

Compatibility is another essential factor. The therapist needs to be someone who can build a rapport not just with the child with ADHD, but with every family member. Some therapists offer an initial consultation for free or at a reduced rate. Use this opportunity to get a feel for their communication style and how comfortable the entire family feels in their presence. It's worth noting that finding the "right fit" might take a few tries, and that's perfectly okay. What's most important is that everyone feels heard and understood.

Location and availability also matter. You'll want to find someone who is conveniently located and has office hours that fit into your family's schedule. Online therapy has become an increasingly popular option and is especially useful for busy families or those living in remote areas. This flexibility can make a big difference in consistency and engagement.

Cost is another aspect to consider. Therapy can be expensive, so it's vital to check whether the therapist accepts your insurance or offers sliding scale fees based on income. Some community centers and non-profits offer affordable mental health services, and larger practices might offer payment plans.

Contact professional organizations for recommendations. The American Psychological Association (APA) and the Children and Adults with Attention-Deficit/Hyperactivity Disorder (CHADD) offer directories and resources that can point you in the right direction. These organizations can also provide information on what to look for in a therapist and questions to ask during consultations.

When considering potential candidates, look beyond the labels and credentials. Pay attention to how they make your family feel and whether their therapeutic goals align with your family's objectives. A therapist who listens, respects, and understands your family's goals will likely be more effective than one offering a one-size-fits-all approach.

It's also essential to set realistic expectations. Therapy isn't a quick fix. It requires time, effort, and consistency. Be prepared to invest in the process, both emotionally and financially. Progress might be slow, but it's the small gains that accumulate into significant changes over time.

Once you've chosen a therapist, maintain open lines of communication with them. Don't hesitate to provide feedback about what is or isn't working. Therapy is a collaborative process, and the therapist's role is to guide and support you, not dictate the terms. Regular check-ins and progress assessments can ensure that everyone remains aligned and moving in the right direction.

Additionally, involve your child in the process as much as possible. When they have a say in picking the therapist and setting goals, they're more likely to be engaged and cooperative. This involvement fosters a sense of ownership and responsibility that can be empowering for children with ADHD.

Finally, be patient with yourselves and each other. Choosing a therapist is a step towards long-term well-being and requires a collective family effort. There will be good days and bad, and that's perfectly normal. Celebrate the wins, no matter how small, and use setbacks as learning opportunities.

In conclusion, finding the right therapist is an essential piece of a much larger puzzle. Investing the time and research upfront to choose wisely will pay off in the long run, setting your family on a path towards better communication, understanding, and overall harmony.

Successful Therapy Techniques

When it comes to family therapy, the road can be winding and filled with numerous obstacles. However, several successful therapy techniques can pave the way for smoother travels. One of the most effective methods is known as "structural family therapy." This approach focuses on the interaction patterns within the family and aims to realign the family structure to ensure healthier relationships and improved communication.

Take, for example, the case of the Johnson family. Meetings with their therapist revealed that the parents often undermined each other's authority, contributing to a chaotic home environment. By helping them recognize and change these patterns, the therapist not only improved the overall family dynamics but also bolstered the efficacy of their parenting techniques. Structural family therapy is particularly beneficial for families with children who have ADHD, as it offers clear guidelines for house rules and expectations.

Another method, known as "cognitive-behavioral family therapy," involves dissecting and reworking negative thoughts and behaviors. This approach is potent because it equips family members with the tools they need to tackle issues head-on. In this type of therapy, families learn to identify problematic thinking patterns and replace them with more constructive thoughts. Through role-playing exercises and real-life applications, cognitive-behavioral family therapy provides a practical, hands-on approach to solving familial strife.

Storytelling is also a powerful tool in family therapy. Techniques like "narrative therapy" encourage family members to share their stories, thereby providing insights into their experiences and emotions. By externalizing issues—seeing problems as separate entities rather than inherent flaws—families can collaboratively work towards solutions. For instance, a child with ADHD might be encouraged to view their impulsivity as a "troublemaker" that can be managed, rather than feeling ashamed of their behavior.

Sometimes, a more eclectic approach is necessary. Combining elements from various therapeutic techniques can often yield significant results. For families dealing with ADHD, therapy might incorporate structural changes, cognitive behavioral adjustments, and narrative elements all at once. This blended approach allows for tailored solutions that address the unique challenges each family faces.

"Experiential therapy" is another avenue that is particularly effective. It relies on activities and experiences rather than traditional talk therapy to facilitate understanding and growth. Activities could range from simple games that reinforce cooperation and communication to more complex exercises that highlight emotional connections. These hands-on experiences often bring underlying issues to the surface faster than conventional methods.

One standout example involves the Davis family, who participated in a weekend retreat filled with team-building exercises. These activities forced them to rely on one another and communicate more effectively. Through experiential therapy, they discovered newfound respect and understanding for each other, which translated into their everyday interactions. Activities like these can be a refreshing break from routine therapy sessions and provide a new lens through which families view their problems and each other.

"Solution-focused brief therapy" (SFBT) is another useful approach, particularly for families eager for quick, effective changes. The focus here is on setting achievable goals and identifying the steps needed to reach them. During sessions, therapists help families draw on their strengths and past successes to foster a sense of capability and hope. SFBT often involves asking future-oriented questions such as, "What will be different when this problem is resolved?" This forward-thinking method keeps the family focused on positive outcomes rather than dwelling on past issues.

When choosing a therapy technique, it's crucial to find a therapist who resonates with the family. The right therapist can make all the difference in the world. For families with children who have ADHD, therapists familiar with the condition can offer specialized strategies and insights, making the therapy process more effective. Credentials are important, but so is the therapist's ability to connect with each family member on a personal level.

Successful therapy doesn't happen overnight, and persistence is key. Engaging in regular sessions and being open to the therapist's guidance play critical roles. It's also helpful for families to practice the techniques they've learned. Repetition and consistency reinforce new, healthier patterns, gradually replacing old, unproductive ones. It may take time, but the results are often worth the effort.

Therapy is not a one-size-fits-all solution. What works for one family might not be as effective for another, and that's perfectly okay. Families should feel encouraged to experiment with different techniques and approaches until they find the right fit. This flexibility ensures that the therapeutic process remains dynamic and responsive to the family's evolving needs.

The ultimate goal of family therapy is not just to resolve specific issues but to equip families with skills and insights they can use well into the future. It's about building resilience and fostering an environment where every member feels heard, valued, and supported. When families commit to the process and remain open to change, the possibilities for growth and healing are virtually limitless.

In essence, successful therapy techniques are as varied as the families who seek them out. From structural changes to cognitive adjustments and experiential learning, the spectrum of options offers something for everyone. No matter the method, the key components remain the same: mutual respect, open communication, and a willingness to grow together. With these principles as a foundation, families can navigate the complexities of ADHD and emerge stronger, more connected, and better equipped to face the future.

So, whether you're considering structural family therapy or leaning towards a more cognitive-behavioral approach, remember that the journey is just as important as the destination. Each step you take brings you closer to a more harmonious family life, and every effort you make lays the groundwork for lasting change. Successful therapy techniques may vary, but their overarching goal is always the same: to build a supportive, loving environment where every member can thrive.

Chapter 13:
Inspirational Stories

There's something uniquely powerful about a good story—one that grips your heart, gives you goosebumps, and perhaps even brings a tear to your eye. Stories have the ability to inspire us, transform our thinking, and motivate us to keep pushing forward, no matter the challenges.

In the complex world of ADHD, it's no different. When dealing with the struggles it can bring to daily life, hearing how other families have managed and even triumphed offers a beacon of hope. Their experiences can be a guiding light showing that, despite the hurdles, success is entirely possible.

Success Stories from Real Families

Let's start with the James family. Sarah and Tom James always knew their son, Ben, was special. Ben's curiosity and boundless energy often left them exhausted but happy. However, as he started school, his inattentiveness and impulsiveness became more than just quirks—they became obstacles. After a long journey of consultations and diagnoses, Ben was confirmed to have ADHD.

At first, the numerous pieces of advice felt overwhelming. Should they try medication, or would behavioral therapy suffice? The James family tried it all—medication, structured routines, and positive reinforcement techniques. There were days when everything seemed to be falling apart. Yet, with every setback, they learned something new.

What worked wonders for Ben was a mix of physical activity and mindfulness practices. They discovered that engaging Ben in martial arts provided not only a physical outlet but also taught him discipline and focus. Combined with mindfulness exercises, Ben started showing significant improvements both at school and home. Today, Ben's teachers commend his spirit and dedication, and his parents couldn't be prouder.

Overcoming Challenges

Another story that sticks out is the journey of the Lopez family. Maria Lopez was close to tears during a parent-teacher meeting. Her daughter, Emma, was struggling academically and socially. She felt guilt and frustration, often wondering if she was doing enough or if she was being too hard on Emma.

Emma's diagnosis brought some relief—finally, an explanation! However, the solutions weren't immediate. They tried various structured routines, positive self-talk exercises, and even dietary changes, but progress seemed slow. The turning point came when Maria encouraged Emma to join a local theater group, something Emma had always been curious about but hesitant to try.

Through theater, Emma discovered a new way to express herself. The practice of memorizing lines and working as a part of a team helped her academically and socially. The discipline and creativity theater fostered began to spill over into other areas of her life. Emma found herself feeling more confident, making friends, and her academic performance also improved.

Maria's key takeaway? Never underestimate the power of finding a passion. Sometimes, all kids need is something they can channel their energy and creativity into. Emma's discovery of theater was pivotal, and today she's not just surviving but thriving.

Celebrating Milestones

Milestones, both big and small, are worth celebrating. The Robinsons made this a core part of their approach when dealing with their son, TJ. Simple achievements that others might take for granted—a good report card, a day without disciplinary issues, or even completing a chore without being reminded—were met with celebrations.

For TJ, the recognition of these small victories was incredibly motivating. His parents adopted a reward system where TJ earned tokens for good behavior and accomplishments. These tokens could be exchanged for small treats or special outings. Celebrating these milestones turned challenges into opportunities for growth and built TJ's self-esteem.

One day, TJ came home with a certificate for "Most Improved Student." This might seem like a minor feat, but for the Robinson family, it was monumental. It signified not only TJ's hard work but also the effectiveness of their consistent, positive approach. It was a day they would recount proudly to friends and family for years to come.

In these stories, common threads emerge—resilience, adaptation, and the unfailing support of loved ones. Whether through martial arts, theater, or small, daily celebrations, each family found their own way to help their child manage and excel despite the challenges ADHD brings.

Every family's journey with ADHD is unique. What's universal, though, is the power of love, patience, and the willingness to try different approaches to find what works best for their child. If there's one thing to take away from these stories, it's that giving up is never an option. Celebrating each milestone, no matter how small, can lead to a brighter, more optimistic future. There will be tough days, but there will also be days of triumph that make the journey worthwhile.

As you navigate your path, remember: you are not alone. Other families have been there and have emerged stronger and wiser. Draw inspiration from their stories, and know that with each step forward, you're building a story worth telling.

Success Stories from Real Families

Emma, a single mother of three, was at her wit's end. Her youngest, Liam, had just been diagnosed with ADHD, and she felt like she was constantly putting out fires. Her house was a whirlwind of activity, and Liam's impulsive behavior added a layer of chaos that made Emma feel like she couldn't catch a break. Desperate for a solution, she attended a local support group for parents of children with ADHD. It was in that room full of empathetic faces that Emma found a lifeline.

The parents shared strategies, resources, and, most importantly, their own stories of struggles and triumphs. Emma realized she wasn't alone, and more importantly, she saw that there was hope. One story that stood out was that of Jack and Diane, a couple whose son, Alex, also has ADHD. They had implemented a structured routine and effective discipline strategies that transformed their home environment from chaotic to calm. Inspired by their success, Emma adopted a similar approach, including visual schedules and positive reinforcement techniques.

The changes didn't happen overnight, but slowly, Emma began to notice improvements. Liam was more focused during homework time and had fewer outbursts. He even started enjoying the new routine, which provided a sense of predictability that calmed his restless energy. Emma's story is one of perseverance and the power of community. She discovered that with the right support and strategies, managing ADHD was not only possible but also rewarding.

Another family that found success through their journey is the Garcias. Maria and Juan were at odds when they first learned about their son, Matteo's, ADHD diagnosis. Maria was in favor of medication, while Juan was vehemently against it. Their differing opinions created tension, making it hard to present a united front in Matteo's treatment. Seeking common ground, they decided to work with a therapist who specialized in ADHD.

Through therapy, Maria and Juan learned to set aside their differences and focus on Matteo's needs. Their therapist introduced them to behavioral techniques that didn't involve medication. One simple but effective strategy they adopted was breaking tasks into smaller, manageable steps. This allowed Matteo to experience small wins, boosting his confidence and willingness to tackle more challenging tasks. They also worked on setting realistic expectations for Matteo, which reduced his frustration and improved his behavior.

Over time, the family dynamic changed significantly. Maria and Juan's relationship improved as they learned to communicate more effectively and support each other. Matteo thrived in the new environment, excelling academically and socially. The Garcias' story is a testament to the importance of teamwork and professional guidance in managing ADHD.

Then there's the story of Sarah and Tom, whose daughter, Lily, struggled with severe anxiety and ADHD. They found it challenging to differentiate between her anxiety symptoms and ADHD behaviors. The constant worry about medication side effects and the balancing act of managing her conditions left them exhausted. In an effort to find a holistic approach, they turned to mindfulness practices.

Incorporating mindfulness into their daily routine was a game changer. Activities like deep breathing exercises, guided meditations, and yoga helped Lily learn to manage her anxiety. This had a positive spillover effect on her ADHD symptoms, making her less impulsive and more centered. The family adopted a nightly ritual of sharing gratitude, which not only fostered a positive atmosphere but also strengthened their emotional connection.

As Lily became more adept at using mindfulness techniques, her self- esteem soared. She was more willing to participate in social activities and less prone to emotional meltdowns. Sarah and Tom's story highlights the value of complementary practices in managing ADHD and the importance of addressing co-existing conditions for a holistic approach to well- being.

One of the most touching stories comes from the Smith family. Janet and Robert Smith were blessed with twin boys, Sam and Ben, both diagnosed with ADHD. The boys had very different manifestations of the condition —Sam was hyperactive and impulsive, while Ben was inattentive and often seemed lost in his own world. The Smiths faced the unique challenge of tailoring their strategies to meet the distinct needs of each child.

Determined to find a solution, they researched extensively and consulted multiple specialists. What they found most effective was creating individualized plans for each boy. For Sam, they incorporated more physical activities into his day to channel his hyperactivity positively. They found that incorporating physical activity like soccer before homework time helped Sam focus better on his assignments. For Ben, they used visual aids and a timer to keep him on task.

The Smiths also placed a strong emphasis on celebrating small victories. Whenever either boy completed a task or behaved well in a challenging situation, they celebrated it with praise and occasional rewards. This approach boosted the boys' self-confidence and motivated them to keep trying even when things got tough.

Over time, the Smith family developed a harmonious routine that catered to both boys' needs. Their story is a shining example of the power of customized approaches and the importance of recognizing and celebrating small steps toward improvement.

Last but certainly not least is the story of Grace, a mother who, after much hesitation, decided to homeschool her daughter, Emily, who has ADHD. Traditional school settings overwhelmed Emily, and her academic performance suffered as a result. Grace worried about her own ability to provide adequate education, but her primary goal was to create a supportive and flexible learning environment for Emily.

They began their homeschooling journey with a curriculum tailored to Emily's strengths and interests. Grace discovered that Emily had a passion for history and art, and they incorporated these subjects into daily lessons. With the ability to take breaks as needed and learn at her own pace, Emily's love for learning was rekindled. Grace also introduced hands-on projects and real-world applications, making learning more engaging and relevant for Emily.

The flexibility of homeschooling allowed Grace to include behavioral strategies that helped manage Emily's ADHD symptoms. Techniques like using a standing desk, integrating physical movement into lessons, and creating a predictable daily schedule made a significant difference. Emily's academic performance improved, but more importantly, her self- esteem and overall happiness soared.

Grace's story is one of commitment and adaptability. By embracing homeschooling, she created a nurturing environment that allowed Emily to thrive academically and emotionally. This journey underscores the importance of finding educational settings that meet the unique needs of children with ADHD.

These stories from real families illustrate that while the journey with ADHD can be challenging, it is also filled with opportunities for growth, connection, and success. Each family found strategies that worked for their unique situations, and in doing so, they not only improved the lives of their children but also strengthened their family bonds. Whether it's through community support, professional guidance, mindfulness practices, individualized plans, or alternative education approaches, there is a path to success for every family dealing with ADHD.

These tales of determination and resilience serve as a beacon of hope and inspiration for others on a similar path. They highlight that while there might not be a one-size-fits-all solution, the right combination of strategies and unwavering support can lead to remarkable outcomes.

Overcoming Challenges

The journey with ADHD is anything but linear, filled with twists, turns, peaks, and valleys. Every family's experience is unique, and despite the myriad of challenges, countless families have forged remarkable paths toward success. It's not about achieving a picture-perfect life; it's about finding strategies that work for you and your family. The stories shared here are a testament to resilience, creativity, and never-ending hope.

Take the Stevens family, for instance. They faced the daunting challenge of getting their son, Josh, through school. Josh's ADHD made traditional classroom settings particularly tough for him. His inability to sit still and focus was often mistaken for misbehavior, leading to frequent calls from school administrators. Josh's parents decided to advocate tirelessly for accommodations tailored to his needs. They worked closely with educators to develop an Individualized Education Program (IEP) that allowed Josh to take breaks when needed and provided him with a quiet space for his activities. This accommodation was a game-changer, turning Josh's academic struggles into genuine successes, one step at a time.

Another powerful story comes from the Martinez family. Their daughter, Sofia, had significant issues with social interactions. She often felt isolated and misunderstood by her peers. During an emotional conversation, Sofia expressed how left out she felt during recess and social gatherings. Her parents' hearts broke, but they didn't let despair take over. Instead, they arranged regular playdates with children who shared Sofia's interests and also involved her in social skills groups. Gradually, Sofia started finding her tribe and even initiated friendships at school. It was a monumental step for a child who once felt so alone.

Emily Jenkins has an inspiring story about fostering a growth mindset in her son, Tyler. Tyler found himself frequently discouraged by the challenges his ADHD presented. Simple tasks like getting dressed or finishing homework seemed insurmountable to him. Emily introduced Tyler to the concept of a "growth mindset," emphasizing that effort and perseverance could lead to improvement. She celebrated small victories with him, whether it was completing a homework assignment or simply following through on a daily routine. Over time, Tyler's confidence grew, and he began seeing obstacles as challenges to overcome rather than roadblocks.

Many families struggle with the emotional rollercoaster that comes with ADHD. There's the constant navigation of high highs and low lows, coupled with feelings of frustration, sadness, and sometimes even guilt. The Harris family dealt with their son, Alex, having frequent outbursts, which put a strain on everyone. They reached a breaking point and sought the help of a family therapist. Through therapy, they learned to identify triggers and employ coping strategies to manage Alex's emotions. Techniques like deep breathing exercises and mindfulness became part of their daily routine. Not only did Alex benefit, but the entire family found a sense of peace and unity they hadn't felt in years.

Johnathan, a teenager diagnosed with ADHD, found his solace in physical activity. Academics were a constant uphill battle, and he often felt inadequate compared to his peers. His parents decided to focus on his strengths rather than his weaknesses. Discovering that Johnathan had a natural talent for soccer, they encouraged him to join a local team. The discipline, routine, and physical exertion of the sport provided a positive outlet for his energy. It also gave him a sense of accomplishment and improved his self-esteem significantly.

Sometimes, the smallest adjustments can lead to profound changes. For instance, the Nguyen family discovered that incorporating short, manageable tasks into their routine significantly helped their daughter, Lily. Instead of overwhelming her with a list of chores or assignments, they broke them down into smaller, specific tasks. This method not only made the tasks seem less daunting but also gave Lily a sense of achievement as she completed each one. It was a gradual yet effective way of building her organizational skills and confidence.

The Williams family had to navigate the challenging waters of medication. Their son, Ethan, had severe ADHD, and while they were initially hesitant about medication, they eventually found it necessary. It wasn't a smooth ride. There were trials and errors with medication types and dosages, each phase bringing its own set of side effects and adjustments. But they stayed the course, working closely with healthcare providers to find the right balance. Ethan's focus and behavior improved significantly, enabling him to better engage with the world around him. The key takeaway: don't shy away from exploring all avenues, even if it's daunting.

Celebrating milestones, no matter how small, is another crucial aspect of overcoming challenges. The Stafford family marked each achievement of their daughter, Katie, with joyous celebration. Katie struggled with speech delays, making it hard for her to communicate with her classmates. When she successfully expressed herself in a complete sentence for the first time, it was a moment of pure elation. These small yet significant milestones became the building blocks for her continuous progress. They served as reminders of how far she had come, fostering an environment of constant encouragement.

There's also the importance of self-care for parents. The Johnsons, parents of twins with ADHD, found themselves exhausted and overwhelmed. They were constantly attending to the needs of their children, leaving no time for themselves. Realizing the toll this was taking on their mental health, they decided to implement small pockets of self- care into their routine. Whether it was taking a few minutes to read a book, enjoying a cup of tea, or going for a short walk, these moments helped them recharge and handle parental responsibilities with more energy and patience.

Ultimately, letting go of perfectionism can be one of the most liberating steps in this journey. The Millers faced this reality when their vision of a spotless home and perfectly organized life came crashing down in the face of ADHD chaos. They learned to embrace the messiness, both literal and figurative, that came with their child's condition. By focusing on what truly mattered—love, support, and progress— they found peace.

It's crucial to remind ourselves that progress isn't always linear, and setbacks are a part of the process. For the Robinson family, dealing with their son's regressions was particularly tough. Just when they thought they had mastered a routine or behavior, they'd find themselves back at square one. Over time, they learned to see these setbacks not as failures but as opportunities for growth. Each regression was a chance to recalibrate and to understand their child better.

These stories illustrate that while the journey with ADHD is fraught with challenges, it's also filled with opportunities for remarkable growth and transformation. The common thread in all these stories is resilience— families that refuse to give up, no matter the obstacle.

Through positivity, strategic planning, emotional support, and sometimes, sheer determination, these families have turned their challenges into inspirational success stories. Each step, no matter how small, is a testament to their unwavering commitment to pave a brighter path for their children.

Celebrating Milestones

In the journey of raising a child with ADHD, it's incredibly important to pause and acknowledge the milestones—both big and small. These moments not only serve as a testament to your child's hard work and resilience but also act as crucial motivators. Milestones can come in various forms, from academic achievements to personal growth in managing emotions or social interactions.

Take, for instance, the story of Daniel. Daniel struggled immensely with his schoolwork and social interactions. Homework time used to be a battle ground, leading to frustration and tears on both sides. However, with a structured routine and dedicated support, Daniel began to improve. The day he brought home his first "A" on a spelling test was nothing short of a miracle for his family. They celebrated with his favorite dinner and a trip to the local park. Such celebrations bolster confidence and mark progress, serving as reminders that while the journey is long, it's also filled with moments of joy.

Another wonderful example comes from the story of Mia, a young girl who found herself overwhelmed by the sensory overload of crowded spaces. Mia's parents decided to celebrate small victories when she started to manage her anxiety better. The first time she managed to stay in the grocery store for a full trip without a meltdown, they treated her to a small toy she's been eyeing. Gradually, Mia began associating these small personal victories with positive reinforcement, making her more confident in facing similar situations in the future.

Recognizing and celebrating milestones doesn't have to be extravagant. Sometimes, a simple heartfelt note or a hug can make all the difference. The important aspect is that it acknowledges the effort and progress, which in turn fosters a sense of achievement and motivation to continue.

One key to celebrating milestones effectively is to be genuine and consistent. Kids with ADHD often have a heightened sense of when they're being patronized or when praise is hollow. Authenticity in celebrating their accomplishments makes them feel truly valued and recognized.

It's crucial to set realistic and attainable goals. Start small—perhaps it's a day where your child successfully follows through on their morning routine without multiple reminders. Recognizing these small steps is huge. It's the daily victories that add up, shaping your child's ability to cope, thrive, and succeed.

Let's consider the journey of Alex, who had difficulty regulating emotions and often lashed out when feeling overwhelmed. His parents worked with him using mindfulness practices and coping strategies. After months of practicing, Alex managed to use his breathing techniques during a particularly stressful family gathering. His parents, recognizing the significance of this milestone, celebrated by allowing Alex to choose a family activity for the weekend. This simple act of celebration reinforced Alex's efforts and encouraged him to continue using the techniques.

Another noteworthy example is the accomplishment Michelle experienced. Michelle had trouble organizing her school materials and often forgot to submit homework. Her parents introduced her to organizational tools and worked closely with her to develop her skills. The first time Michelle handed in all her assignments for a week, her family decided to celebrate with a movie night. This acknowledgment helped Michelle realize the benefits of being organized and spurred her on to maintain her new habit.

Speaking of unique methods, some parents create achievement boards where children can visually track their progress. Stickers, stars, and colorful markers transform these boards into vibrant displays of success. Every star on the board serves as a visual affirmation of their hard work and progress.

Celebrating milestones isn't solely reserved for monumental achievements. It's the daily, incremental progress that often goes unnoticed but deserves recognition. Saying "I noticed you completed your chores without being asked – great job!" can go a long way.

And let's not forget the importance of community in celebrating these milestones. Sharing successes within your support network can provide additional validation and encouragement. Whether it's a support group or a close-knit group of friends, surrounding yourself with a community that understands and celebrates your child's progress can be invaluable.

School achievements, such as improved grades or a positive report card, are often celebrated with gifts or special outings. However, personal growth milestones deserve equal recognition. Elijah's story is compelling for this reason. Elijah struggled with peer relationships and found it challenging to make friends. His parents encouraged him to join a club that matched his interests. The day Elijah confidently approached another child to join him in a game was a milestone worth celebrating. They marked the event with a small party featuring his favorite treats and games, which further encouraged Elijah to continue building friendships.

Reflecting on these stories, it's evident that celebrating milestones instills a sense of accomplishment and encourages persistence. For children with ADHD, the promise of recognition can be a powerful motivator. The key is to celebrate consistently and genuinely.

By focusing on both academic and personal growth milestones, parents can help their children recognize their own potential. Celebrating a child's ability to manage their emotions or successfully following a routine carries just as much weight as celebrating academic achievements.

Take into account the story of Sam, who had difficulty understanding social cues and interacting appropriately with his peers. With ongoing guidance and practice through role-playing scenarios, Sam began to show improvement. The first time he navigated a social interaction without prompting, his parents chose to celebrate this major milestone by allowing Sam to have a playdate with a friend of his choice. Such positive reinforcement encouraged Sam to continue improving his social skills.

Ultimately, celebrating milestones isn't just about the immediate reward. It's about fostering an environment where effort is recognized, and progress is valued. This cultivates a growth mindset, where challenges are seen not as insurmountable obstacles but as steps in a larger journey.

Every inch of progress signifies resilience, perseverance, and capability. Celebrate these moments authentically and regularly. They create an ongoing narrative of success and possibility. In this way, celebrating milestones becomes not just a practice but a cherished tradition in the journey of raising a child with ADHD.

Conclusion

As we come to the end of this journey together, it's clear that navigating the world of ADHD is much like solving a complex puzzle. Each chapter of this book has provided a piece, a critical insight or actionable tip to help you craft a strategy that's effective for your unique situation. You've taken the time to understand what ADHD is and dispelled common myths and misconceptions that cloud judgment. Recognizing the unique brain structure and function of a child with ADHD sets the stage for the empathy and patience required for positive parenting.

By embracing positive parenting principles, you're empowering your child with the skills they need to thrive. The power of positivity is undeniable. Setting realistic expectations ensures that you're not demanding the impossible, but rather celebrating progress, no matter how small. Fostering a growth mindset encourages your child to see challenges as opportunities and setbacks as stepping stones.

Building strong relationships is the core of any successful strategy for managing ADHD. Effective communication and emotional connection cannot be underestimated. Your child needs to feel heard and valued. Trust and respect form the bedrock upon which all your efforts will stand.

Consistency brings a sense of security that's particularly vital for children with ADHD. Developing daily schedules and creating routine give structure to their day, reducing the chaos that can often exacerbate symptoms. Transition techniques help ease the stress that can come with moving from one activity to another.

Effective discipline strategies harmonize boundaries with freedom, guidance with space. Positive reinforcement encourages the behaviors you want to see more of, while natural consequences impart life lessons without the need for punitive measures. Setting clear and firm boundaries ensures that your child knows the limits and understands the repercussions of crossing them.

Supporting academic success involves more than just homework help. It's about working collaboratively with educators to create an environment where your child can excel. It's teaching organizational skills that will serve them for life. Celebrating small victories in the educational arena boosts confidence and fuels a desire to learn.

Empathy is a cornerstone skill in encouraging social competency. Role- playing scenarios can bring the abstract into tangible practice, strengthening your child's ability to navigate social interactions successfully. Inclusion in social activities provides opportunities to apply these skills in real-time, fostering a sense of belonging and building lasting friendships.

Self-esteem is a fragile thing, but with careful nurturing, it can blossom. Celebrating strengths rather than focusing on weaknesses allows your child to build confidence brick by brick. Positive self-talk combats the inner critic, creating a resilient mindset.

Managing emotions is an ongoing process, a dynamic interplay of recognizing triggers and employing coping strategies. Mindfulness practices bring a sense of calm and control, teaching your child how to navigate the storms of strong emotions.

The decision to navigate medication can be one of the most challenging choices for any parent. Understanding the options, weighing the pros and cons, and working closely with healthcare providers ensures that if medication is part of the solution, it's done thoughtfully and responsibly.

Incorporating physical activity into daily routines is beneficial both physically and mentally. Finding activities that your child enjoys ensures they stay engaged and derive immediate pleasure. It's all about balance, ensuring that activity levels are high enough to release pent-up energy but not so high that they become another source of stress.

Family dynamics play a pivotal role in the ADHD journey. Selecting the right therapist and employing successful therapy techniques can dramatically alter the course of your family's experience. Therapy provides a safe space to explore feelings and work through challenges collectively.

The inspirational stories shared by real families highlight resilience, determination, and the full spectrum of human emotion. They remind us that while the journey can be difficult, it's also filled with victories worth celebrating. These stories serve as beacons of hope, validating your experiences and inspiring perseverance.

If there's one takeaway, it's this: You're not alone in your efforts. With the practical, actionable advice from this book, any challenge can be met with hope and resilience. The path may not be easy, but it is navigable, and the rewards of seeing your child succeed are immeasurable.

In conclusion, this isn't just about managing ADHD; it's about fostering a loving, understanding, and supportive environment where your child can thrive despite the challenges. It's about seeing beyond the label and recognizing the incredible potential each child possesses. Parenting a child with ADHD requires patience, creativity, and unwavering support, all of which are within your reach.

Your compassionate journey through this book has equipped you with an arsenal of tools and techniques. You've shown up for your child by seeking out resources and educating yourself. As you move forward, remember that each small step counts and each act of love amplifies in ways that create lasting change. Here's to your child's success and the fulfillment of your role as a loving and empowered parent.

Appendix A:
Appendix

Welcome to the appendix, an essential resource that rounds out the content of this book with additional tools and references. Here, you'll find carefully curated resources and support networks to help guide you and your family on this journey. Take advantage of these materials as you continue to build a supportive environment for children with ADHD.

Resources and Support Groups

Seeking support is an essential part of managing ADHD effectively. Below is a list of organizations and groups that offer valuable information and assistance:

- **CHADD (Children and Adults with Attention-Deficit/Hyperactivity Disorder)** - A national non-profit organization providing education, advocacy, and support for individuals with ADHD (*www.chadd.org*).

- **ADDA (Attention Deficit Disorder Association)** - Focuses on the needs of adults with ADHD and provides resources for managing symptoms across the lifespan (*www.add.org*).

- **Understood.org** - Offers a wide array of resources, including expert advice, practical tips, and a supportive community for parents of children with ADHD (*www.understood.org*).

- **ADHD Support Groups on Social Media** - Various Facebook groups and forums offer peer support and shared experiences from others dealing with similar challenges.

Recommended Reading

Enhance your understanding and approach to ADHD with these insightful books:

- **"Driven to Distraction" by Edward M. Hallowell and John J. Ratey** - This best-seller offers a thorough look into understanding ADHD and practical advice for those affected by it.

- **"Parenting Children with ADHD: 10 Lessons That Medicine Cannot Teach" by Vincent J. Monastra** - Provides actionable strategies rooted in experience and research for managing ADHD in children.

- "The ADHD Workbook for Kids: Helping Children Gain Self-Confidence, Social Skills & Self-Control" by Lawrence E. Shapiro - **Features engaging exercises to help children develop key skills for managing ADHD.**

- **"Taking Charge of ADHD: The Complete, Authoritative Guide for Parents" by Russell A. Barkley** - This comprehensive guide is packed with vital information every parent needs to help their child thrive.

We hope these resources and readings empower you with additional tools and knowledge. Remember, the most significant steps often come from sources beyond the pages of a book. Engage with communities and seek support through shared experiences. The journey may be challenging, but you are not alone, and these resources are here to help you every step of the way.

Resources and Support Groups

In our journey of supporting children with ADHD, finding the right resources and support groups can be a game-changer. Whether you're looking for firsthand experiences, expert advice, or merely a sense of community, there are abundant options available that cater to various needs. Let's dive into these invaluable resources that can help guide you through your day-to-day challenges and celebrations.

First up, let's talk about local support groups. Local groups can be incredibly beneficial as they provide a space where you can connect face- to-face with others who are going through similar experiences. Many communities offer these groups through schools, community centers, or even local hospitals. The advantage of local groups is the personal interaction and the opportunity to build friendships with other parents and caregivers. Additionally, some groups may host guest speakers from fields like psychology, education, or healthcare, providing a wealth of information tailored to your community's specific needs.

National organizations dedicated to ADHD can be invaluable. The most well-known ones include CHADD (Children and Adults with Attention- Deficit/Hyperactivity Disorder) and ADDitude. CHADD offers a membership that includes access to a vast library of articles, webinars, and an annual conference that's a treasure trove of expertise. ADDitude, on the other hand, is an online magazine that frequently publishes articles from leading ADHD specialists, offering practical advice that's easy to integrate into your daily routines. Both organizations also offer forums where you can connect with other parents and caregivers.

Speaking of online communities, the internet hosts a plethora of forums and social media groups where you can find support at any time of the day. Websites like Reddit have forums dedicated to ADHD, where members share their personal stories, advice, and resources. Facebook also has numerous groups focusing on various aspects of ADHD, from parenting tips to medication discussions. These online spaces can be particularly helpful for those who perhaps don't have access to local groups or prefer the anonymity that online interactions can provide.

Books and literature also serve as an excellent resource. Many renowned experts have penned insightful guides that offer both scientific explanations and practical advice. Titles such as "Driven to Distraction" by Dr. Edward Hallowell and Dr. John Ratey or "The Explosive Child" by Dr. Ross Greene, provide in-depth knowledge that can help you understand ADHD better and develop effective strategies to address its challenges. Including a few good reads on your bookshelf can both educate and inspire you.

Don't overlook podcasts as a resource; they're a fantastic way to absorb information during your commute, workout, or even while doing household chores. Podcasts like "ADHD Experts Podcast" from ADDitude and "The ADHD Podcast" by K8t are packed with interviews from top specialists and cover a broad array of topics—from emotional regulation to the latest in ADHD research. They provide an easy-to-digest format for busy parents who might not have the time to sit down with a book or article.

Webinars offer another dynamic way to gather valuable information. Many national organizations and local support groups host webinars featuring experts in the field. These webinars can be attended live, allowing you the chance to ask questions directly, or they can often be accessed later as recordings. This can be particularly advantageous if you're interested in very specific topics or need professional guidance without the expense of an in-person consultation.

Therapists and coaches who specialize in ADHD can provide tailored support. These experts can work with individuals and families to create customized strategies that address unique challenges. An

ADHD coach can help with everything from organizational skills to emotional regulation, while a therapist might assist with underlying psychological challenges. Finding the right professional can make a significant difference in how effectively you can manage daily life and long-term goals.

Your child's educational environment is another critical resource. Engage with teachers, school counselors, and educational psychologists who can provide support tailored to your child's academic needs. Schools often have resources such as Individualized Education Programs (IEPs) or 504 plans, designed to accommodate students with ADHD. Understanding these resources and advocating for your child's needs can set them up for success not just academically, but socially and emotionally as well.

For those considering holistic approaches, alternative therapies such as occupational therapy, nutrition counseling, and even mindfulness programs can offer additional layers of support. Occupational therapists can help with sensory processing issues, while nutritionists can assist in developing a diet that supports focus and well-being. Mindfulness programs can teach children techniques for self-regulation and managing anxiety, which often coexists with ADHD.

If you're overwhelmed by the sheer volume of information out there, it may be helpful to create a personalized resource guide. Start by listing the resources most relevant to your situation and gradually expand as you become more comfortable. This approach allows you to focus on immediate concerns while keeping an eye on future needs. Consider including contact information for local support groups, recommended books, useful websites, and the names of specialists you've consulted or plan to consult.

Last but not least, never underestimate the power of personal networks. Friends, family, and even coworkers can be sources of support and information. Sometimes sharing your experiences can prompt others to share their own advice, leading to unexpected yet invaluable resources. Building a network of trusted individuals who understand your situation can provide emotional support that is just as crucial as any formal resource.

In summary, resources and support groups are essential allies in managing ADHD, providing everything from expert guidance to emotional support. Whether you tap into local communities, national organizations, or online forums, the key is to stay connected and continually seek information that resonates with your needs. With the right resources, you're better equipped to foster environments where children with ADHD can thrive.

Recommended Reading

Finding the right resources to support your journey with ADHD can feel like searching for a needle in a haystack. To help you navigate this challenge, we've compiled a list of recommended readings that offer practical advice, inspirational stories, and advanced insights tailored for compassionate learners like yourself. Below, you'll find a variety of books that cater to different aspects of ADHD, ensuring that you have a comprehensive toolkit at your disposal.

First and foremost, let's talk about foundational knowledge. If you're new to the world of ADHD, understanding the basics is crucial. Books like "Driven to Distraction" by Dr. Edward M. Hallowell and Dr. John J. Ratey offer an engaging introduction. These authors, both of whom have ADHD themselves, provide insights that are both scientifically grounded and deeply personal. Their anecdotes and narratives will resonate with your experiences, making the information easier to digest.

For those looking to delve deeper into the intricacies of the ADHD brain, "The ADHD Effect on Marriage" by Melissa Orlov is an excellent choice. Although it focuses on adult relationships, it provides invaluable insights into how ADHD affects interpersonal dynamics. This book can help you understand potential challenges and offer practical strategies for managing them, which can be applied to various relationships, including those with your children.

Next, consider expanding your understanding of positive parenting principles. "The Explosive Child" by Dr. Ross W. Greene is a must-read. Greene's approach emphasizes collaboration and problem-solving, which can be transformative for both you and your child. It aligns with the themes discussed in Chapter 2, focusing on setting realistic expectations and fostering a growth mindset.

Creating structure and routine is another critical area that can significantly impact children with ADHD. "Smart but Scattered" by Dr. Peg Dawson and Dr. Richard Guare offers practical strategies for developing executive functions in children. The book includes tools and techniques for creating effective routines, which can be seamlessly integrated into your family's daily life. This ties in perfectly with the strategies discussed in Chapter 4 about developing daily schedules and transition techniques.

When it comes to effective discipline strategies, "1-2-3 Magic" by Dr. Thomas Phelan is a game-changer. It provides a straightforward, easy-to- implement framework for managing difficult behaviors without resorting to punishment. This aligns well with the concepts of positive reinforcement and natural consequences discussed in Chapter 5.

Supporting academic success is another crucial area where expert advice can make a world of difference. "The Homework Machine" by Dan Gutman isn't just an entertaining read for kids but also subtly addresses the challenges of homework. While it's a fictional narrative, it can be a great conversation starter with your child about their own homework habits, tying into the more structured advice available in "The Organized Student" by Donna Goldberg and Jennifer Zwiebel.

Social skills are essential for building strong relationships, as high-lighted in Chapter 7. "How to Win Friends and Influence People for Teen Girls" by Donna Dale Carnegie takes Dale Carnegie's timeless principles and adapts them for a younger audience. It offers practical advice on teaching empathy and social inclusion, which are crucial skills that will benefit your child throughout their life.

Boosting self-esteem is another area where targeted reading can offer significant benefits. "You Are a Champion: How to Be the Best You Can Be" by Marcus Rashford provides an empowering narrative that encourages children to celebrate their strengths and build confidence. Rashford's journey from a challenging upbringing to becoming a successful athlete serves as an inspirational tale, perfectly aligned with the themes discussed in Chapter 8.

Managing emotions can be particularly challenging for children with ADHD. "The Whole-Brain Child" by Dr. Daniel J. Siegel and Tina Payne Bryson is an excellent resource that offers strategies for recognizing triggers and implementing coping strategies. The book's approach to mindfulness practices aligns well with the techniques discussed in Chapter 9.

When navigating medication options, it's crucial to have a comprehensive understanding. "ADHD: What Every Parent Needs to Know" by the American Academy of Pediatrics provides a balanced overview of various treatment options, including medication. It addresses the pros and cons and offers guidance on working with healthcare providers, complementing the insights provided in Chapter 10.

Incorporating physical activity is another vital aspect of managing ADHD. "Spark: The Revolutionary New Science of Exercise and the Brain" by Dr. John J. Ratey dives into the numerous benefits of exercise. It provides compelling evidence on how physical activity can enhance brain function, reduce symptoms of ADHD, and improve overall well-being. This book offers practical advice on finding enjoyable activities and balancing activity levels, aligning with the themes in Chapter 11.

Family therapy can offer immense support and guidance for families navigating ADHD. "Raising An Emotionally Intelligent Child" by Dr. John Gottman is a fantastic resource that provides insights into family dynamics. It emphasizes the importance of emotional intelligence and offers practical strategies for successful therapy techniques, complementing the discussions in Chapter 12.

Finally, inspirational stories can offer hope and motivation. "The Gifts of Imperfection" by Brené Brown is a powerful read that celebrates imperfections as strengths. While not solely focused on ADHD, this book's message of self-compassion and resilience resonates deeply with families facing ADHD challenges. Brown's narrative style and her ability to connect on an emotional level make this book a valuable addition to your reading list, aligning with the themes of success stories and celebrating milestones discussed in Chapter 13.

With these recommended readings, you'll have a wealth of knowledge at your fingertips. Whether you're seeking practical advice, inspirational stories, or advanced insights, these books offer valuable perspectives and actionable strategies. Remember, the journey with ADHD is unique for every family, but with the right resources, you're well-equipped to navigate the challenges and celebrate the successes along the way.

www.ingramcontent.com/pod-product-compliance
Lightning Source LLC
Chambersburg PA
CBHW020419290526
45785CB00002B/639